ADVENTURES IN MANIFESTING

ADVENTURES IN MANIFESTING

SOULFUL RELATIONSHIPS

Sarah Prout and Sean Patrick Simpson

The Adventures In Manifesting series: Volume #6.
First published 2013 by Älska Publishing

Office based in Melbourne, Australia

Typeset in Giovanni LT 9/12/14 pt

© Sarah Prout and Sean Patrick Simpson

The moral rights of the authors have been asserted.

National Library of Australia Cataloguing-in-Publishing entry:

Authors:	Prout, Sarah 1979 – / Simpson, Sean Patrick 1984 –
Title:	Adventures In Manifesting: Soulful Relationships
ISBN:	9780987162946 (pbk) 9780987162953 (ebook)
Subjects:	Self help, New Age Publications, Inspiration
Dewey Number:	158.1

Cover design by Sarah Prout

Editorial revisions in house

Printed in Hong Kong

Also available in electronic format

www.AlskaPublishing.com

Wholesale Discounts
For competitive rates on bulk purchases, please go to www.AlskaPublishing.com

Disclaimer
The material in this publication is of the nature of general comment only and does not represent professional advice. To the maximum extent permitted by the law, the authors and publisher disclaim all responsibility and liability to any person, arising directly or indirectly from any person taking or not taking action based upon the information in this publication.

Älska means to LOVE

(Say it like this: *elsh-ka*)

This book is lovingly dedicated to all the soulful relationships in our lives.

CONTENTS

Conclusions

GRATITUDE

With the deepest gratitude, we would like to thank all of the Älska authors for sharing their incredible and inspiring stories in this book. We would also like to thank our students of **TheManifestingCourse.com, AdventuresInManifesting.org,** and *you* (the reader) for supporting the Älska vision of Love and Oneness.

From Sean:

Whenever I think of my own soulful relationships, I am immediately overwhelmed with a deep sense of love for the friendships I've developed. To my crew, my friends from Mt. SAC, and my soul family (you all know who you are), this book would never have been possible without you. Thank you for being my teachers.

To Dallyce and Scott, you may be across the world, yet you are always so near. Thank you for everything you are.

To my eternal love—Miss Sarah Prout—flying to Australia for those 11 days was one of the best decisions of my life. By the time this is in print, you will finally be my wife. To Thomas and Olivia—you two have taught me about an entirely new level of soulful relationships I couldn't thank you enough for!

To Mark, Amr, Francis, Russell, and Gemmalou—your integrity, work ethic, and quality of work is extraordinary. Sarah and I are blessed to have such a magnificent team. Thank you to the entire Adventures in Manifesting and Verbii.com team!

To Mr. TP and Miss HP, I frikkin' love you guys! Big hugs Daddy-O and Sistah! To Mom and Dad—thank you for all of your support!

To those whom I made spiritual agreements with before this life but have now parted ways with—*thank you* for giving me the essential lessons I've needed to grow consciously.

From Sarah:

To Scott and Dallyce for being on the other end of the phone when "everything" "always" seemingly turns to shit, your love and support means the world to me. Thank you from the bottom of my heart and spiritual toolbox.

To Sean—my twin flame, best friend, business co-pilot, and husband: I love you. Words cannot express how much you have taught me about soulful relationships. You are my biggest mirror, and I feel so blessed to be able to spend forever with you.

Thomas, Olivia, Cookie and Merlin—people say not to work with children and animals, but I think you guys are the best souls on the planet and I adore you with every fiber of my being. Thank you for choosing me to be your mummy.

Special hugs to Tony, Louise, Hetta, Shae, Lauren, and Roger, thanks for the best gift ever! Thanks also to Bronya, Amber, Joy, Evelyn, my SPROUT mastermind students, and you (the reader) for supporting the vision for Adventures in Manifesting.

INTRODUCTION

Älska

It is with soul-felt gratitude that we would like to welcome you to the *Adventures in Manifesting* series. It has been designed as a source you will continuously enjoy reading when in search of insight, wisdom, and inspiration. The stories are shared from people just like you that are on a wondrous journey of self-discovery.

From a multitude of unique vantage points, these stories demonstrate active examples of inner guidance, connection, faith, and love that have transcended all limitations. Each story has been written with you in mind.

Reading With Your Soul

Our advice to you is that you read with an open heart, an open mind, and absorb the information that sparks your own adventure in manifesting. When reading from a place of wonderment and curiosity, you are bound to find deep resonance. Ask yourself, "What here resonates with me? What inspired action am I being guided to take? What can I learn from this now?"

Allow yourself to find a connection point within each story and within yourself that is right for you.

Your Own Treasure Map

While you will discover truths that each author has found for themselves, you can find in-between the lines your own truths as well. The wonder of this book is that understanding and resonating with certain concepts will happen at different points in your life. So take your time.

Keep the book by your bedside table. Pick it up when you feel inspired, and follow your inner guidance to the story you're meant to draw from now. Whether you read through it all in one sitting or piece-by-piece, you will find this a place of inspiration for years to come.

The Mission of Älska & Verbii.com

The mission of Älska is to bestow the teachings of love and oneness and proliferate its message throughout the world. Within these two illuminated concepts is the power of vibrancy, creativity, joy, and inspiration. While the mechanisms of metaphysical principles here have been in place since the dawn of time, it is our purest intention to continue this work that began to gain prominence at the beginning of the nineteenth century in the New Thought Movement.

Our mission is to offer a powerful platform for people to share their stories with the world. And, thus far, we have hundreds of authors in over thirty countries with chapters in the *Adventures in Manifesting* series, as well as manuscripts self-published through Verbii.com.

What are You Manifesting?

You may have noticed on the front cover this very powerful question. Ask yourself this to begin reading with some basic intentions and ideas of what you desire. Just as we would teach you, we are *acting as if* and actively demonstrating how to imprint the Universe with the vibration of success, thus the questions.

In the years before Jim Carrey became a superstar, he wrote himself a check for $10 million and added "for acting services rendered". He carried it in his wallet from that day forth until the abundance and recognition that he desired started to manifest in his life. This act of setting an almighty intention contributed to his success eventually growing to fruition. As witnessed, the Universe responds to what is radiated energetically.

Your Journey Begins Now

Start it from a place of love and gratitude, knowing that as you read you will find resonance with what you are in alignment with in this point of time.

You will find yourself beginning to develop a story through direct experience of your intended reality. As you do, we will be here waiting with expectant joy and an open heart to see what you have to share with the world as well.

Until then, we will look forward to hearing all about your own adventures in manifesting.

With Love and Gratitude,
The Älska Publishing Team

About Älska

Älska is the combined energies of Sarah Prout and Sean Patrick Simpson. The company name means *Love* and was received as gentle guidance one evening after a very intense session of laughter and joy.

You say it like this: 'elsh-ka' – which is slightly different than the original Scandinavian pronunciation of their verb (which means *to love*).

Sean and Sarah were prompted from within to start a metaphysical publishing company based on their mutual adoration of Universal truth and passion for writing. Hence, Älska was created and has since expanded into several brands and start-ups that continue to blossom in the entrepreneurial space.

http://www.AlskaPublishing.com
http://www. Verbii.com

GET YOUR FREE MANIFESTING WORKBOOK!

Discover an *ancient manifesting technique* you've probably never even heard of before...

www.TheManifestingCourse.com

Share Your Experience

Has a particular story, insight, or teaching stood out to you?

We'd love to hear about your experience, so feel free to get in touch and let us know. You can e-mail us at:

feedback@adventuresinmanifesting.org

Additionally, with the intention and desire to share stories and teachings from all walks of life, we'd like to invite you to potentially be a part of one of the next *Adventures in Manifesting* titles.

Stories of all topics about manifesting are welcome (success, spirituality, health, happiness, wealth, love, prosperity, inner guidance, achieving dreams, overcoming obstacles, etc.).

If chosen as a top submission, we will get in touch directly to invite you to be a part of one of our next *Adventures in Manifesting* titles.

Please go to www.AdventuresInManifestingSeries.com to share your experience (not to mention join the course and community, as well as find the hard copy, Kindle, and iBook versions of other titles in the series).

THE DIVINE REASON YOU'RE WORTHY OF TRUE LOVE

Sarah Prout and Sean Patrick Simpson

Sarah's Perspective

"You'd never leave me! Who's going to love you with that wrinkly skin around your belly?"

The arguments my ex-husband and I had during the 10 years we were married tended to be pretty fierce. Trying to be as hurtful as possible, he would resort to throwing the nastiest insults he could: from 'slut' to 'whore' to 'princess bitch, too precious to wipe her own arse,' I heard it all.

Not entirely blameless, I dished out a fair share of cruelty during our time together as well.

What I didn't realize is that throughout the 10 years I was married to this man, the insults were slowly corroding my sense of self and well-being.

Diary entry 13ᵗʰ of December, 2004 (Gothenburg, Sweden)

I feel so awful. Not that I want to affirm it, but why do I feel so terrible? It's been 3 months since I had a period. I'm not pregnant and I'd really like to be. I chew my nails all the bloody time and don't want to.

How can I stop?

I must have no respect for myself. I fight with my husband, I'm mean to my son, I hate my body and I'm never motivated long enough to achieve anything. I'm such a sack of shit. I'm 25 and would love to have a life filled with sunshine, friends my own age, challenges and laughter. I fucking hate myself and I am so fucking lazy. I want to go home but wherever I go I still have to deal with myself.

I'm so depressed. I hate you Sarah Prout.

I loathed myself. I was trapped in a cycle of self-rejection and fear of being alone. I felt damaged, broken, and rather than taking responsibility for my own wellbeing, was constantly looking to my loved ones to "make" me happy.

That year I became virtually bulimic for eight months. With a damaged throat, I spoke with a raspy voice due to the fact I had been burning the inside of my mouth.

From the outside I looked like a seemingly contented housewife. But behind closed doors I would watch 7 hours of television per day, shower in the dark so I wouldn't have to look at my disgusting body, clean the house just before my husband arrived from work, and feel guilty when I needed to ask him to watch our son so I could go to the supermarket.

I felt as though absolutely *nothing* was working in my life and that *everything* was out of balance. Feeling empty, invisible, unhappy, depressed, sad, lonely and angry—that was me on a daily basis—and every night, I would secretly plot my escape.

Fast forward nearly 9 years to September 2013…

It's been 4 years since I first separated from my husband and 3 years since I met the true love of my life, Sean Patrick Simpson. As of the 21st of September, 2013 (two weeks after writing this chapter) we will be married at an exquisite hotel in Las Vegas, Nevada. And we will be surrounded by the type of friends, family and loved ones I had always wanted.

While the love story Sean and I share is truly unique, there is an energetic transaction we have that *anyone* can attract for themselves if they have the right spiritual tools to identify if they're on the right track.

During my 10-year marriage, I didn't begin developing that toolbox until the near end, after I started taking steps to create my own business. Only then did I begin to feel the faintest murmur of empowerment starting to emerge as I focused on serving others, turning my self-hatred into gratitude, and actively focusing on personal and spiritual development.

As my business grew and my soul slowly began to blossom, I started seeing the need for my marriage to end. And as painful as it was, I can now see that it was all part of a journey where every skerrick of pain served a purpose.

When looking at this realization from a high level overview, you can see that all pain is part of a greater lesson – a journey mapped by your soul for you to grow. Without the dark nights of the soul, how would we learn to appreciate the light?

You see, you are part of an exquisite fabric of Oneness. A sublime counterpart in a bigger picture that facilitates your soul's growth and expansion. All relationships are a vehicle towards superconsciousness, and you are manifesting expansion for your soul on a daily basis through *all* the people you interact with.

All these people are mirrors. And they are mirrors that can help you learn and discover one of the most beautiful gifts in life. That gift is the understanding that the core layer and foundation of all soulful relationships, is the relationship you have with yourself in relation to the Divine.

After the traumatic catalyst for the ending of my marriage had completed its cycle, I knew it was time to move on. I just knew. And with every fiber of my being, I set an extremely powerful intention to change my life. Getting really clear about what I wanted to create for myself, I set the goal to leave my marriage. On the Friday, I had nothing. And by the following Monday afternoon, I had manifested $12,000 to start a new life with my kids.

Taking that leap was one of the most empowering steps toward freedom, and I really believe the Universe rewarded me for being brave enough to stick to my guns and solidify my intentions. Since then, I have created a beautiful relationship with myself—a joinery of falling in love with who I am (with all of my flaws) and learning to laugh at the "Divine Comedy" we call life.

Within less than a year of first tasting the blissful freedom of living life on my own terms and taking care of myself for the first time, I managed to manifest the man of my dreams on Twitter (check out *Adventures in Manifesting: Love and Oneness*). But here's the thing: when Sean arrived in my life, I was still in the process of managing my grief, learning how to be "Sarah Prout" and not "Mrs. So-and-So". It was my commitment to *loving myself first*, that allowed me to attract him into my life.

When you consciously acknowledge that you are worthy of love—all forms of love (self-love, romantic love, platonic love, blissful Divine love)— life begins to get super sweet. You feel alive, wonderful and understand that your life's journey has prepared you for where you are right now, which is perfect.

Sean is the closest person I have ever met that is almost identical to me in every way. He is my mirror, and with that understanding, we know and can consciously acknowledge that we have put our hands up to do some pretty intense spiritual work, based on our mission as publishers and as husband and wife. . . .

When you can identify that you have consciously chosen to manifest pain so that you can blossom into a much greater, stronger, and more vibrant soul for this very short time we are permitted to walk the earth, you'll see that it's all such a grand illusion designed as a veil. Once that veil is lifted, you'll see that we are all animated by the same force that created us. We are *Love*.

Sean's Perspective:

For as long as I can remember, my life has been about attracting meaningful connections into my life and creating deep, soulful relationships.

To explore soulful relationships though, we must first ask ourselves, what *is* a soulful relationship? Is it the love shared with a partner, a family member, a friend?

I believe the depth and diversity of soulful relationships are infinite. Each person has their own unique definition of what it is and how they are created.

Personally, I believe that soulful relationships extend beyond people's love and connection and embrace the pain and heartbreak they experience as well. Relationships, no matter how loving, aren't void of challenges or struggles. They are intertwined with them as great teachers. And that's where the beauty, magic, and depth reside—in both the harmony and the dissonance. The light and the dark.

Think of the most gorgeous sunset you've ever seen. . . .

What is it that makes it so beautiful?

Is it the light that glistens through, or is it the darkness that softens the sky?

Within every sunset are different shades of light, color, and darkness: a beautiful array of colors that mix and match to create different patterns and experiences.

So is the same with relationships.

Soulful relationships are simply those ones that we use to grow and expand (rather than contract) spiritually and guide us back to love.

As we grow spiritually and ask our higher selves how we can learn from every experience, we continually create more opportunities to paint the sunrises and sunsets that we most desire for our relationships. There will, of course, still be waves and tides that come in when we least expect. What's great is the spiritual growth we experience through diverse relationships empowers us to create a spiritual toolbox of new and more empowering energetic responses to each situation.

Loving Unconditionally

For a long time I questioned what it actually means to love unconditionally.

How can you love someone that's hurt you? How can you love in the midst of pain?

What I've come to realize is that it's not about the experience of loving in every single moment. It's about the intention to have love as your center and the heart-space you actively come back to. My step-children have been wonderful teachers for me of how to love unconditionally.

Having unconditional love doesn't mean you don't get hurt or angry or upset. What it means is that you've embraced the awakened consciousness that *love is all there is*, that *I am love*, that *I will express love as much as I can*, and that *I will continue to come back to love* if you've strayed away from it.

Loving thy Self

Experiencing love in its fullest form requires more than loving in one direction (externally). It's about loving in the other as well (internally). It means embracing self-love.

When we acknowledge that love is all there is, we can even go beyond this internal/external metaphor and realize that love is omnidirectional. It is everywhere and in everything, as everything.

If you desire to experience the richest, most fulfilling soulful relationships, then realize your own divinity and embrace the fact that *everything about you is worthy of love, and it begins by choosing to love yourself.* By doing this, you are able to love without conditions and love without compromise. You are able to love without judgment and even love when being judged.

The key is to stay true to yourself. Stay true to your soul. In the end, everyone wins. . . . Even those with deep insecurities do. They either experience the self-growth they need, attract into their lives what keeps them in their comfort zone, or grow to a new level of consciousness.

Loving with All Your Heart

You've picked this book up for a reason: likely because you want to create more soulful relationships or embrace the ones you already have.

Whatever the reason, I'd like to leave you with this.

Choose to love fully, deeply, and completely. Every day, in every single moment, you have this opportunity. Set the intention and do your best to love with all your heart. And when you find yourself incapable, just remember who you really are deep down inside and what's at your heart's core: *Love.*

Knowing what you *really are* is the quickest way to finding your way back and being able to love unconditionally without judgments or compromise.

There *will* be times you are out of the flow. And there will be times you are in the flow...

The beautiful thing about life is that all these experiences are here for a reason. They are here to give you the beautiful contrast between day and night—the sunrises and sunsets. And they are here to give you the opportunity of fully appreciating the magnificence that is life. The magnificence that is love.

Every experience is here to guide you. Every experience is here to expand your soul and show you new possibilities.

It's up to you to see and embrace them with all that you are. . . .

Love.

About the Authors

Sarah Prout and Sean Patrick Simpson are bestselling authors, new media publishers of the *Adventures in Manifesting* series, and creators of Verbii. com, the self-publishing platform for conscious authors. Their authentic and charismatic approach to teaching metaphysical studies has inspired students around the globe. With a strong social media fan base, the twin-flame couple have shared their joyful journey with thousands.

Together they believe in the power of connection to engage an audience from the screen to the stage. Their mission is to teach others how to create a life filled with love and how to manifest their dreams.

You can connect with Sarah and Sean personally, as well as the other authors and readers of this book through the Adventures in Manifesting community.

http://www.adventuresinmanifesting.org
http://www.sarahprout.com
http://www.verbii.com

CULTIVATING EVERYDAY PRESENCE: LEARNING TO LOVE ALL OF LIFE

Dallyce Brisbin

*"The heart is like a garden. It can grow
compassion or fear, resentment or love.
What seeds will you plant there?" – Jack Kornfield*

For many of us, it is not until we experience the loss of our external choices that we discover what true freedom is. The good news is, we don't have to wait for tragedy or drama to strike to free ourselves from illusion. Every single time we shift our internal perception from one of fear to one of love, we cultivate our freedom. The opportunity to plant new seeds and watch what grows is always available to us, and our loving Soul has no preference for what we cultivate—any relationship or situation is deemed worthy of the label "Soulful" in the eyes of our Spirit—it's our fearful little ego that is the picky one!

My very first relationship in this world continues to be the longest running, deepest, and most Soulful Relationship of my life. My relationship with my mum has provided the framework for me to experience a lifelong demonstration of what unconditional love (which I define as giving love freely without expecting anything in return) really is. No matter what comes up for me, she's always there if I need her. She has celebrated my joys and cushioned my sorrows. She's always made room for me to make mistakes, and, no matter how poorly I've treated her at times, she's never turned her back on me, especially in my many hours of need. She's saved my life more times than I can count. Literally.

My dad is my second longest running connection and we, too, have a profoundly deep and Soulful Relationship. He is an optometrist and my mum is a teacher, so they've both spent the majority of their lives studying and working with perspective. One of the most valuable lessons Mum ever taught me is that, ultimately, the only thing I have any real control over in life is how I choose to perceive and respond to whatever is happening in *this* moment. Dad taught me that the lens through which I view things makes a huge difference in whether I see them with clarity or distortion. This turned out to be incredibly valuable information for me to have access to early on, and I am grateful for all the lessons they've shared with me on the subject.

Life plans and weather forecasts have a lot in common. Despite our best efforts and predictions, life and storms can take unexpected turns. No amount of planning, forecasting, visualizing, or preparing can change that. Like most people, I've weathered unexpected storms throughout my life—some big, some small. While preparation and planning can certainly be helpful in moving through daily life more smoothly, when the unexpected happens and we enter uncharted territory, it is incredibly valuable to trust the clarity of our perspective in the present moment so we can accurately and efficiently navigate through even the most difficult experiences.

I came into this world with a weak immune system. It started out as mostly minor ear, nose, and throat stuff, but year after year my health continued to deteriorate. Snuffles and colds as a toddler slowly developed into chronic bronchitis and chronic pneumonia, which eventually became full blown asthma by age ten. I was eleven the first time my mum had to give me mouth-to-mouth because my asthma attack was more than my medication could relieve. She would end up giving me mouth-to-mouth literally thousands of times. No amount of planning could have prepared our family for what would become a major part of our daily lives for the next several years. The medications that were keeping me alive were also shutting my body down. Doctors were in an ongoing struggle to find the right balance without killing me one way or the other. We faced the very real probability every day that it could be my last, and we had many extremely close calls.

Vivian Greene's quote, "Life isn't about waiting for the storm to pass; it's about learning to dance in the rain," has become one of my guiding principles for my life and relationships. It reminds me to make friends with whatever or whomever shows up in my life and to look for the opportunity or treasure hidden inside whatever style of packaging each life experience comes wrapped in.

I was twelve the first time I had to have an IV. I was terrified of big needles, and had I been given the choice, I would have chosen several days in bed on oral meds rather than a few hours and some discomfort. I clearly remember that day my doctor came in and told me I was just too sick this time and would have to have an IV. I was scared, mad, and felt very trapped. I felt like I had no control over my own life. Little did I realize this experience of external immobility would become one of my greatest classrooms for exploring consciousness and playing with perspective.

The day I got that first IV, my mum shared this life-changing lesson with me: "While you may not be able to choose what happens *to* you, you do get to choose *how* you respond to it, and a simple shift in perspective has the ability to radically change your experience of whatever situation you find yourself in." She said, "Even when the going gets tough—and it will get really tough at times—the opportunity to choose a different perspective is *always* available, even if you've already chosen a less empowering perspective."

Serious illness has the ability to act as an express lane for recalibrating our perceptions if we let it. When we can't easily change the channel on the outside of our experience, we always have the option available to either stay stuck in our version of an awful nightmare or to start playing around with the dials of our internal experience. If we choose the latter, we soon discover a whole new style of programming that can transform whatever is playing out in our external situation and make it a whole lot more tolerable. When I started to peel apart the eternal (I Am . . . Love) from the temporary (this is . . . fear), I found that all forms of fear were really just temporary storms that pass through my experience. Some were small, some were massive; but, regardless of their intensity, they were temporary.

Since we both knew this was likely going to be the first of many, *many* needles and IVs to come, my mum and I created a game I could play to make the situation more bearable. I would rate the nurses on a scale of 0-10 for every needle I got. Zero meant they really sucked, and ten meant they were so skilled that I couldn't feel the needle going in. Little by little, with each needle I received over the days and years ahead, I began to appreciate just how much my attitude affected my experience—and, often, I discovered, it could even shift the response or attitude of the other person!

Don't get me wrong, I had a ton of crappy days where I chose to hold tightly to my fear and frustration. And for the record, I *still* have my share of crappy days, though they are far less intense than they used to be. Fortunately, I was never made to feel "wrong" when

I made that choice, and I'm grateful for that because it gave me the opportunity to explore my whole experience and consciously choose for myself. Allowing ourselves to really feel our fears provides immensely valuable feedback. My mum has a beautiful capacity for compassion, which always made it easier to move myself through my "stuckness" more quickly. The compassion she demonstrated for me back then served as a framework for me to cultivate self-compassion, which is a tool I use daily.

Whether I'm engaging with an annoying telemarketer or laughing with my amazing husband, I find that the less preferences, rules, and expectations I tie to my experiences, the more room there is for me to find joy, love, wonder, and adventure. Through trial and error, I've learned that whenever I focus on cultivating flexibility, fluidity, adaptability, and creativity within myself, I'm able to weather the various storms of life much better when they come barreling through.

Cultivating those skills also allows me to embrace the full spectrum of life and all of its colorful characters. I've come to see every relationship as a soulful relationship. Some are smooth and easy, some take effort and attention, some really stir up my pot, revealing an assumption I've been harboring just below the surface of my consciousness.

In Canada, we have a cough syrup called Buckley's. Their slogan is "It tastes awful. And it works." I often think of that line when I find myself with someone whose personality isn't one of my favorites. Buckley's reminds me that although not all flavors of spiritual nutrition are tasty, every interaction has the potential to strengthen my soul's constitution.

Similarly, I've learned that no matter how abusive someone is to me, or how much I dislike or disagree with a particular point of view, ultimately, no one can force me to respond in a certain way. That is *always* my choice. This is definitely easier said than done, especially at the beginning, but like any new skill, it takes practice before it becomes a habit. Cultivating love instead of fear, especially because we are bombarded with fear messages daily, takes consistent effort and attention, and it can feel overwhelming if we think that not getting it "right" 100 percent of the time means failure. When I finally realized this isn't just a class we go through once and either pass or fail, I was able to relax and become gentler with myself. I find it helpful to think of it more like washing the windows in my house or cleaning the lenses of my glasses on a regular basis so I can see things more clearly.

As a caveat, I want to be clear that I am not suggesting that anyone remain in any situation that is not serving them if they are able to make a change. What I am saying is that I believe there is not one person in the world, no matter how distorted their perspective and behavior, whose heart isn't seeking love and trying to ease its pain.

Viktor Frankl, an Austrian neurologist and psychiatrist as well as a Holocaust survivor, said, "Between stimulus and response there is a space. In that space is our power to choose our response. In our response lies our growth and freedom."

Whatever physical action we take or decision we make is much less important than the *mindset* we hold when we make that decision to take that action. Are we reacting, or responding? When we are able to access the space in between whatever stimulus triggers us and the response we choose, we can literally shift the way we perceive the world. That space he is referring to *is* the present moment, and our experience of life expands whenever we are able to see that every single person and situation is offering us the same opportunity— the opportunity to choose our thoughts and our actions consciously from the present moment and not through the filtered lenses of the past or future. Another way to look at this is that *Responses* are made from our Soul's perspective, and are rooted in the present moment. *Reactions* are made from the ego's perspective, and are rooted in the past or the future.

Practically speaking, I've found that any time I get caught up in the thick of some drama or fear, it can be really tough to see very clearly in that moment. So, over the years, I've cultivated some simple, easy-to-use reminder tools that have made it easier for me to make room for presence so I can begin to make a shift from perceiving my current experience through a lens of fear to a lens of love.

I find that funny metaphors or games (like the one my mum and I came up with rating the nurses in the hospital) with the ability to conjure up a combination of physical sensation and visual image are most helpful. They seem to break up the intensity of the pattern and playfully bypass my mind chatter. The humor aspect is designed to truly "crack" me up! Laughter softens tough exteriors.

It also acts as an express lane back to my awareness of the present moment, where I am able to access a greater perspective and make a more conscious choice. Below are a few examples to demonstrate what I mean.

Reminder Tool #1—Any Upset is a *Rules* Upset

Remember on Sesame Street when various lessons would be sponsored by certain letters? *Today's Lesson is brought to you by the letter R and the letter S!*

Well, I used that concept to create some playful indicator lights for my inner dashboard to alert me when one of my subconscious rules believes it has just been challenged or violated.

The first metaphor I use is to imagine my body as the shape of a capital letter R. Whenever I feel my body taking on some aspect of that shape, such as my chest sticking out with my arms crossed tightly, my back getting rigid, or my legs moving into a bracing stance, or when I feel all twisted up (the sign language symbol for the letter R is the index finger and third finger wrapped around each other), that tells me that one of my "Hard R's"—AKA my Rights, wRongs, Rigid Rules, Reactions—have been activated, and that's my cue to relax and revisit the underlying belief! It's amazing how quickly this tool can get me back on track.

The letter S also provides a fun visual cue that can quickly shift my focus. I imagine my body as a stick of butter. Whenever I feel my body stiffening up or notice my thoughts becoming solidified or hardened, that lets me know that I need to metaphorically take myself out of the fridge and soften myself up. Why? Because *Soft butter Spreads Smoothly*, which tastes *So much better* when paired with the bread of life!

My main purpose for creating these quirky reminders was to have some simple, fun tools to remind me to dance with life rather than fight it. I've always found humor to be a great way to loosen things up and get things moving again. I encourage everyone to have some fun and create some metaphors that can lighten things up when they find themselves stuck. Life is too short to be serious!

Reminder Tool # 2—I am Responsible For My Own Interpretations, Responses, Actions, and Interactions

Years ago, I learned an experiential metaphor from Debbie Ford that I continue to find very helpful—when we point one finger out in blame, we have three pointing back at ourselves. Just like the wind makes waves on a lake, sometimes my emotional state can make it difficult to see what is just below the surface. But if I tune inwards and wait for the weather to pass, I eventually can see what curious creature is lurking down there. Whenever I perceive that someone has done something to me, I take a closer look at how I've tried to justify my behaviors using other people's actions as an excuse for my conduct. Then I am able to see where I blew right through the space between the stimulus and the response that Viktor Frankl talks about.

Self-compassion is key to releasing or sustainably transforming any habit. The Dalai Lama said, "To be aware of a single shortcoming within oneself is more useful than to be aware of a thousand in somebody else." So, on days when I'm feeling courageous, one of my exercises for strengthening my self-compassion and expanding my perspective is to revisit a time when I judged someone harshly or shared something about another person that was peppered with my personal opinion. I look for places that I was more interested in grasping or clutching onto my own point of view, and then I begin to trace it backwards to find the source of fear or pain that it was highlighting within me. This is an incredibly enlightening exercise and one of the most powerful forms of clutter clearing I have ever experienced. It has become a joyful adventure exercise for me. And the cool thing is there is a never-ending supply of material to work with!

Reminder Tool # 3—Mistakes, Assumptions, Judgments, and Fears Make Great Compost:

Oscar Wilde once said, "Experience is the name everyone gives to their mistakes." If that's the case, then I am well versed in how to gain experience! Honestly, I'll take experience over theory any day. We learn and grow through trial and error. Direct experience is the only way to discover what is true for each of us. Life is one big feedback system, constantly responding to our input. The key is learning how to accurately interpret the results, and what specifically we throw into the petri dish is irrelevant.

When we are able to truly understand what is being reported back to us, our decisions on which beliefs are truly serving us and which ones are ready to be moved on to the compost pile becomes clear. Why do I like the analogy of the compost pile? Because when viewed through a lens of wholeness, *everything* has value. Even our stinky thinking! Rotting matter may not smell great, but it's an essential ingredient for compost, which creates nutrient rich soil for new seeds to grow.

Cultivating perspective, compassion, and soulful relationships are all interconnected. Any time I am able to loosen up my expectations and keep my inner critic in check, I increase my opportunities for experiencing learning, growth, and joy, while minimizing my odds of suffering significant disappointment.

One thing every single person on the planet has in common is that we are all human! When fears and judgments surface, we can soften them by reminding ourselves that, while we may or may not ever act upon something, we are certainly *capable* of making the same choice as the person we are judging.

The truth is that we can never truly know what decision we will make in a certain situation until we find ourselves actually in it. Remembering this allows me to make space for compassion and empathy and to bypass my mind's craving to make assumptions.

Cultivating self-compassion over self-esteem can create enough spaciousness between stimulus and response for me to look honestly at my choices and behaviors and evaluate what's still fresh and what is past its "best by" date! This imagery metaphor makes me laugh—and often makes it easier to see when it's time to move some outdated belief, assumption or rigid rule out of my daily operations and over to my consciousness composting pile.

There are still plenty of times in my life when I don't walk my talk and when I judge others, say hurtful things, clutch tightly to my habituated fear-based thoughts, and make decisions that do not serve my highest and greatest good. And, of course, there are also lots of times when I am just plain lazy! The less I judge myself, the more willing I am to see that the times I mess up, fall short, or don't make the effort are also learning opportunities. I can learn a lot if I'm open to seeing it through a wider lens than just my current limited point of view. It all works synergistically—no real beginning or end: just a continuous cycle.

I see myself very much as a work in process, and these are just some of the tools I currently use to help keep myself from wandering too far from the middle path.

Cultivating our perception is a lot like driving or sailing or gardening: it is a dynamic and constantly changing experience. We are not static creatures, so why should our perspective be? Who I am today is not who I will be tomorrow, so while these lessons are still fresh and nutritious for me today, my perspective or their usefulness to me may change tomorrow. As I evolve, so does my perspective. This is why I am a big fan of direct experience over theory. What is true for me may not be true for you. So please don't take my word for anything - and don't take anyone else's word for anything either. Give yourself a gift and put an end to the habit of making assumptions. Cultivate the practice of doing your own due diligence in every area of your life. If something I've shared appeals to you, take it, try it on, and see if it fits. Make alterations to it if you like, or toss it out. I make no claims to be an expert on anything. I am simply a fellow traveler, asked to share with you one of the routes I have explored so far and what I discovered along the way.

Ultimately, all journeys and relationships end up in the same place. Right here, right now. Regardless of whether you are enjoying a spectacular sunrise or gasping for your last breath, all of life happens *now*. Our recording of each memory has nothing to do with what is actually happening moment to moment and everything to do with how we choose to perceive it and label it.

Loosening my grip on how I think life "should be" allows much more room for "what is" to bloom. When I view the cultivation of Everyday Presence as my creative medium, I'm open to using whatever unfolds in my life situation as my seed. The present moment becomes my soil and my attitude becomes the water and the sunshine. From this perspective, I can trust deeply that I will always be able to enjoy a clear view through life's window, looking out on its rich and diverse landscape, actively blooming with colorful wildflowers, regardless of my physical surroundings.

The storms of life aren't within our control. But whether we see them as obstacles or opportunities is completely up to us. We can choose to perceive them through a lens of fear or love. We can choose to wait for the storms to pass or we can work with what's here in this moment and learn how to dance in the rain. We can endure what life offers us or we can embrace it.

The choice is always ours.

About the Author

A meditation mixologist, consciousness adventurer, spiritual nutritionist, groovy wife, rockin' dog mum and devoted student of Life, Dallyce Brisbin is also an engaging author, entertaining speaker, and effective mentor. She combines relevant information, personal experience and humor to share lessons she's learned about the incredible regenerating capabilities of the human heart, body, mind and spirit. She is the founder of EverydayPresence.com and offers programs to help people discover their innate ability to experience more joy, love, wonder and adventure in every life situation. She is also co-owner of Destiny Training Systems, a Conscious Business Consulting firm dedicated to helping clients cultivate soulful business relationships and improve their triple bottom line: People, Planet, Profit.

http://www.EverydayPresence.com

UNSTOPPABLE LOVE

Bob Doyle and Lynn Rose

Lynn:

It's 2006. Suddenly, everyone, including *Time Magazine, Oprah,* and *Good Morning America,* is talking about the same film: *The Secret.*

"See it—it will change your life!"

I'd heard about it before its release, as I personally knew many of the transformational leaders featured in it. It did impact millions—but it touched me in one specific way I could never have imagined at the time. . . .

Like most, I watched in fascination and appreciation and, then, on came Bob Doyle. His humorous and humble style was appealing (not to mention his boyish good looks), but I felt something much deeper strike me right in the gut. It felt almost crazy—a visceral feeling of "knowing" him.

After the movie, I combed the internet, curious to learn more. That is where I discovered he was married with kids. *Wow!* I didn't want to believe it. But I could and would never cross that line. I had to choose to let the powerful feeling go.

I went about my own life, but, through the years—from afar—whenever I'd see something Bob Doyle was releasing, I'd still strangely feel that familiar pull.

It would spark me wondering about that special kind of partnership I longed for; however, instead, I found myself going from relationship to relationship, making wrong choices that wrought havoc in my personal life and, if anything, took me off my higher path.

It left me thinking: "Maybe real love's not meant for me?"

Bob:

At twenty-two, I got married right out of college. In retrospect, I can say that while my heart was in the right place, I was far too young and ill-prepared for the commitment. I hadn't yet discovered who "Bob Doyle" really was, but I stepped right into the role of husband and father.

Fairly early into the marriage, though, it was clear that although the woman I had married was amazing, this marriage was not right for me.

I did my best.

But rather than acknowledging that I simply wasn't ready and we weren't the right match, I felt something must be "wrong" with me.

On and off for years, I sought every possible type of advice: program, books, and even endless counseling around my inability to bring the same level of commitment and passion that my wife was able to.

Deep inside, however, I knew the truth: I wanted and needed out. But I had the overwhelming belief that leaving the marriage would cause so much pain for her, my kids, and me, that I would not be able to survive it.

So, for years and years I did nothing.

The irony is that by continuing to do what I thought was the "right thing", I ended up causing even more damage. Yet, despite the struggles in my marriage, I was still able to create amazing things in other areas of my life.

I had become a focused, committed "seeker", which eventually led me to becoming a leading expert in the Law of Attraction and being one of the featured experts in *The Secret*.

Because of the success of the film and book, I was suddenly "popular", sought out by men and women from all around the world. It was a whole new experience. It made me all the more aware of the life I wasn't living . . . the connections I wasn't making . . . all because I felt trapped.

This ended up leading to more resentment and anger at myself. My kids witnessed more fighting than ever. My health began to suffer. My business began to die on the vine. I found I wasn't feeling creative or inspired in any area of my life (talk about the real "Law of Attraction").

One day, in the midst of all this, I came across a video called *Everybody*.

Tweet featuring Lynn Rose.

I had never heard of her but was instantly taken by her playfulness, talent, energy, and beauty. But it made me sad to think that if I were ever to meet a woman like Lynn, it would always be impossible to do anything about it if I were still allowing my fear to keep me paralyzed and stuck.

So I continued to wonder, "Maybe the kind of love I've longed for is not meant to be for me?"

Lynn:

Flash forward to 2011. I was supporting my friend, Cynthia Kersey, in her mission to create sustainable communities in Africa through her Unstoppable Foundation. That night was her annual Unstoppable Gala, with over two hundred of the leading transformational experts, authors, and speakers in attendance.

I was busy conducting red carpet interviews, herding attendees, and slated to sing for the event. *Darn if I hadn't neglected to choose my own seat!* So I had to grab the nearest chair at a table where I didn't know anyone.

Or so I thought. . . .

That's when I turned and saw *him*—Bob Doyle—sitting right at my table! How fascinating! But he was different than how I remembered him. He seemed stressed, serious, and distant.

I wasn't looking for anything romantic, though, as I'd just gotten out of a relationship that had broken my heart, and, besides, he was married and I wouldn't go near that. Still, it was great to meet him in person.

We exchanged a few words about exploring working together as so many of us in our industry were typically discussing that night. Then duty called, so I had to rush off to sing the song to kick off the official festivities and got caught in the swirl of activity the rest of the evening.

Bob:

The first time I saw Lynn in person was at that Unstoppable Gala.

Ever since the *Everybody Tweet* video, I had considered Lynn an unapproachable celebrity, even though I had reached a level of professional recognition myself from *The Secret*.

When I saw Lynn at the event, interviewing VIPs on the red carpet, I unexpectedly felt my heart leap in my chest.

At that time, I was in a particularly deep funk about my marriage and carried the heaviness around quite visibly (as I later heard from several people).

After the VIP reception, it turned out by accident (divine providence?) that Lynn sat at the same table. Intimidated, I found myself trying to think of something to say that wouldn't make me look like an idiot.

While the idea of continuing communication was definitely exciting, I was afraid of the conflict and drama a friendship with her might cause at home.

As I watched her singing and getting the crowd moving, she was mesmerizing, but of course, my circumstances wouldn't allow us to form the close type of relationship I'd idealized, so I sadly let it go. For the most part. . . .

Lynn & Bob:

With Bob in Atlanta and Lynn in LA, a distant industry type of friendship began. . . .

After a year had passed, Bob emailed industry peers that he was looking for partners in doing a retreat, and Lynn was one of the ones who responded.

Together they decided to offer retreats around the US based around "transformation through play"—*an idea that got us excited to work together!*

They planned to shoot footage for their promotion at Lynn's studio on that Monday, following the next upcoming Unstoppable event, as Bob would be in town at that time.

Lynn:

Now, it's the Unstoppable Gala 2012. I was busy again interviewing on the red carpet and helping to organize the flow.

I barely had a chance to even say *hi* to Bob in the midst of the flurry of activity.

Soon, it was time for me to kick off the dancing after the fundraising. I invited everyone to the dance floor to dance to *Edge of Glory* as I sang—one of my best *ever* performances!

As I left the stage, Bob Proctor, Marcia Weider, and others raved, and Bob even ran up to congratulate me.

I was happy to see him and very much looking forward to filming our segments together on Monday. I could feel that familiar tinge of secret longing but had to instantly let it go (yet again).

Bob:

On the evening of the 2012 Unstoppable Gala, one of the first things I did was seek out Lynn.

Even then, it was apparent we had mutual admiration going on, and I was excited about the prospect of finding more time to talk with her.

But the reality remained: I was still married, even years after I'd known I needed to move on, because of the ever-present fear of hurting people.

So, although I was excited about spending the retreat planning time and shooting promotional videos with Lynn, I carried the burden of immense guilt and resentment.

That Monday we spent in the studio, however, was magical. Our natural chemistry on camera was immediately evident. We found we even shared the same offbeat sense of humor.

When I had to leave that Monday to head back home, something in my heart had opened up, but I made a promise to myself that I would *not* burden Lynn with sharing what was going on in my marriage.

And, of course, I had to leave with everything still platonic.

Lynn:

That Monday in the studio filming with Bob was surprisingly off the charts. We instantly clicked on camera, and I also secretly felt a personal chemistry but had to stuff it away into the unspoken.

In the ensuing months of planning the project, our friendship deepened, and I found that Bob was real, caring, funny, wildly creative, and, of course, brilliant.

Then I ended up getting involved in a different, demanding project that fell onto my lap, which completely put my progress with Bob on hold. In the rare moments we touched base, I wondered what was happening on his end, as he was often distant.

When Bob finally confessed he was in the throes of marriage troubles, I encouraged him to do what felt right for him while making sure he'd tried everything he could to save the marriage. I'd even tried connecting him to a relationship counselor.

As our friendship deepened, however, Bob shared how he had stayed in his difficult marriage for years, how he had tried everything, and how his staying stuck had been causing wear and tear on his business, not to mention his sense of self.

Bob:

At home, the fighting had escalated.

Reluctantly I began to share about how I was suffering—how my fear had me paralyzed in every area of my life.

Lynn (a natural "coach") reflected back to me things I already knew, as so many others who'd offered advice before had. Lynn was wonderfully supportive, with no "agenda" other than me reclaiming my own power.

One night, I finally saw the divine perspective of the damage I'd been doing to everyone in my family by staying.

I'd known for years that I'd given one hundred percent to endlessly trying to fix it and I had become years overdue to leave.

It was time.

So, in late May of 2012, amidst incredible pain, anger, and sadness, I moved out . . .The process of rediscovering myself and a long road to healing had finally begun.

Soon after, an event was to bring me back to Los Angeles, where Lynn lived. So we made plans to reconnect at her studio to continue creating the videos we needed to promote our planned retreats.

So here I was with Lynn again, only now I was free to express my feelings.

I had no idea how swiftly these feelings would escalate now that my situation had finally changed.

Here's the fascinating part: I had told myself for years that once I was out of the marriage, I would just have fun and avoid a serious relationship like the plague for the foreseeable future. The *last* thing I thought I wanted was a "committed relationship".

I learned, however, that all of that changes when you meet "The One".

It happened so fast and, yet, we found we both had such a deep "knowing" about not only our current feelings, but also about a shared vision of the future.

Our situation was not without serious challenges, however; it was about the stress and pain around the dissolution of my marriage, horrendous financial issues, and the strain on my business. My children were hurt, angry, and confused, especially because of how quickly things happened with Lynn, right after the break-up, and there were even accusations about her role in the leaving of the marriage (which had nothing to do with her).

On top of all this, Lynn and I had become business partners, launching a business from scratch and with wildly contrasting, creative approaches.

To avoid hotel costs, I had to live with Lynn whenever I was in LA. So on top of everything else, we had practically jumped into living together, which any relationship counselor would warn against.

Now, *any* one of these situations could have torn any normal couple apart; yet, the love and bond we innately shared not only somehow endured, but actually grew as we went through every challenge in both the relationship and as individuals.

My most profound shift above all came when, to my surprise, I began to experience and realize commitment as *freedom* instead of imprisonment . . . a freedom that is born of profound trust in each other and that deep knowing.

I now feel completely safe to be one hundred percent Bob Doyle, with all the imperfections, while holding the space for Lynn to do the same.

We uplift and hold each other to a higher standard and forgive each other when we fall short.

She is my best friend, my lover, my partner, and my Muse.

Lynn:

I'd never have known what being with "The One" really means and what real love is if it hadn't been for Bob.

Before, I'd run from a relationship when it would hit the tough times or if I felt someone getting too close.

But when it's "The One", everything changes. Come to find out, it doesn't mean a fairytale fantasy. It means an opportunity to grow and expand. It means the "knowing" is stronger than the toughest, most unimaginable challenges.

It's the knowing that had me stay even though my normal pattern would have been to leave. And the reward of choosing to stick by the 'knowing' is not only the deeper, loving, natural relationship with Bob, but is also its amazing life lessons.

I get to see my own issues in full color in how they're reflected back to me. I also get to *see* and *know* Bob for who he *really* is—even underneath the reactive swirl he would get caught in from the multitude of issues he ended up going through.

My *knowing* was telling me that this is a good man who's been through so much and is healing right now.

My *knowing* was saying that the dynamic between Bob and me can be a force for good in helping launch and transform others.

Bob fully accepts me for all of who I am, too. And the real freedom is that shared gift of trust. I have one hundred percent trust in his commitment to us and to our vision together.

Having a partner who "gets" me, who loves me unconditionally, who's got my back, and who's committed to us, growth, and honest communication is the ultimate!

And it's not about romance book cover fantasy. It's about real friendship and meaningful partnership and a divine coming together that makes both of us better people and better available to serve the planet with our shared purpose.

We should have been torn apart by what we went through, but we *both* consciously chose and were led by the *knowing* over any circumstance we faced.

We now reap the rewards of having survived and navigated through it together.

Bob & Lynn:

At the Unstoppable Gala 2013, Bob and Lynn now walk the red carpet together as a couple. They did so well with their business they launched together, they were even able to bring in two sponsor tables and it feels so good to help such a great cause together.

When Lynn is called onstage, she sings from a yet even deeper place.

Bob gets to watch her performance as her partner now. He is so grateful that he finally, *finally* had the courage to honor his heart and knowing and manifest a kind of love he'd always wondered if he could ever know or have.

As Lynn comes offstage and into his embrace, they are so grateful for the gift of who they are, what they plan to bring to the world, and, most importantly, for the divine gift of their unstoppable love.

About the Authors

Lynn Rose is a transformational speaker, singer and TV host, having spoken or performed for hundreds of thousands of people around the world and continuing to ignite audiences globally when she speaks or performs.

She is the go-to trainer for experts on her WOW Process for speaking fearlessly, authentically, and powerfully, called "The WOW Factor".

Bob Doyle was one of the featured experts in the movie *The Secret* and is the creator and facilitator of the Wealth Beyond Reason Law of Attraction curriculum. Partnered with Lynn, they help experts get positioned as top of their industry.

http://www.lynnrose.com
http://www.wealthbeyondreason.com
http://www.launchyounow.com

EMBRACE THE WOMAN IN THE MIRROR

Irene Elias

When you find your beloved inside you,
you will find your beloved beside you. – Alan Cohen

I was a highly sensitive person—an angelic girl who was a target for being bullied and manipulated. My high school experience was torturous for me. Each day I had to face the bully. I couldn't understand why I wasn't able to stand up for myself and why no one believed me. Many nights, I would cry on my bedroom floor, hugging a teddy bear, and promising myself that it would be the last time I would allow anyone to hurt me, only to disappoint myself over and over again. This led to self-loathing and suicidal thoughts.

All I wanted was to be accepted exactly as I was.

At the age of seventeen, a man whom I trusted and adored forced me sexually. I blamed myself for this happening and for not being vocal enough and strong enough again. I also talked myself into believing that I, too, wanted this to happen. I figured who would believe me anyway, just like the story of the bully—I was the sensitive girl who didn't have a voice.

Eventually, into my late teens, I wasn't so angelic after all—I figured being who I was wasn't getting me anywhere, so I also became a bully to protect myself and went down the destructive path of food binges, alcohol, smoking, and boys to drown my insecurities and pain.

My self-worth was deteriorating.

One fateful night, at the age of nineteen, vacationing with my sister, I was to meet a charming man from Hollywood who was a literary agent. He made me smile, laugh, and said all the things any girl would hope to hear from a guy. In that one night of partying with him, it seemed liked he was my answered prayer to my wounded heart. We kept in contact for two years and spent hours on the phone, talking about everything and anything. He sent me love letters, and surprise gifts, and I finally felt validated, accepted, and listened to.

Was this possibly my prince in shining armor who was going to complete me?

I had just turned twenty-one and wanted more from my life. I had dreams to become a dancer and I also wanted to explore the world. So I decided to go to Los Angeles. In hindsight, I was running away from my problems and hoping to be saved by my prince in shining armor who promised me the world.

My first couple of months felt like I was living a dream. I was taken to Hollywood parties, meeting celebrities, walking on red carpet, going behind movie sets, dining at funky restaurants and hanging out at Venice beach. I was living like most girls would dream of. But what they didn't know and what I was to discover, was that it wasn't like the movies. Hollywood wasn't so glamorous after all, and fame, money, and looks definitely didn't equate to happiness.

Surrounded by body-image obsession, I became extra paranoid with how I looked and didn't feel I was thin or pretty enough. This began to chip away at my self-esteem.

My relationship with my prince seemed to be growing as we opened our hearts to sharing our hopes, dreams, fears, and secrets. He continued with his romantic antics and made me feel like I was the only girl in the world. As time went by, I began to notice warning signals and red flags in his behavior. But I chose to ignore them and made excuses for him because of his dysfunctional upbringing.

A few months later, my prince charming surprisingly proposed to me while we were on vacation having dinner on the beach. I was speechless. So much uncertainty was going on in my head, and I heard a loving voice in my mind say, "No, don't do it."

In every moment, decision, or challenge in our lives, the voice of our soul guides us toward the right direction, but, until we awaken to this deeper spiritual connection, this voice is ignored.

"Aah!" I screamed out loud as I fell backwards in my chair and onto the sand. I had no idea how I fell; I guess that was my other sign. We both started laughing as he grabbed my hand and helped me up. I chose to ignore that voice and agreed to marry him.

We were both broken and blinded and the relationship was doomed to fail from the get go.

A couple of months after our engagement, each day my prince would slowly reveal his true mask. From a prince, he turned into an abusive and possessive partner with a Dr. Jekyll and Mr. Hyde personality. He would swing back and forth from being abusive and then to being the most loving and caring man. This is what would confuse me about him. One minute I was treated like gold and the next like dirt.

All my feelings that I ran away from, all seemed to be coming back to greet me head on, but more intensely. Never in my wildest nightmare had I ever imagined myself to be abused mentally, verbally, emotionally, and sexually by my partner.

My wishful fairytale had turned into a nightmare. And my prince, whom I thought I fell in love with and whom I thought loved me, was not real. It was all a façade. I was confused, scared, stuck, lost, and powerless. With not an ounce of self-worth or self-esteem left, I remained in the co-dependent relationship and kept forgiving him under his hypnotic spell. I was a complete mess in my size zero frame.

At any time I had a choice to leave but I was unconscious and in a haze how the Universe worked.

Four years later, a month before my wedding, the puzzle of my fiancé all seemed to come together. I was to discover he cheated on me and was leading a double life filled with betrayal. Fearful of where my life was headed, one night when he wasn't home, a power of something greater gave me the strength and courage to collect some pieces of my self-worth and self-esteem off the floor so that I could take charge of my life and run away from the relationship. I ran to my parents' home.

When he found out I'd escaped, he tried to put on his charming mask again to fool me into coming back to him. When he didn't get his way, he became abusive and threatening. My life seemed to become like the movie *Sleeping With the Enemy*. He came to my hometown and began stalking and harassing me. I felt I was going insane. In that moment, I truly could understand how one could drive someone to a mental institution.

Being at home was also reminding me as to why I left in the first place. So I decided to run away again, this time to New York, carrying all my unresolved fears, wounds, insecurities, relationship issues, hatred of men, and bad habits with me, hoping to bury my past and start anew.

I was a victim and had no idea as to why all of this had happened to me. I was disappointed with the world, myself, and God.

I continued looking outside of me to validate my self-worth. Soon, I was to meet a caring and loving man. But how was I to trust any man again? And how was I to trust myself? Nonetheless, we became close friends and I caved in and told him everything about my past. Whenever I would open my heart to him, his eyes would just swell up in tears. I felt there was something different about this man. He became my alley, my support, and what I called my Earth Angel.

My nightmare wasn't going to end that quickly. My ex-fiancé had hired a private investigator and discovered where I lived in New York. I bleached my hair blonde so I could try and change the way I looked and try to faze out the memories of my past, which haunted me every time I looked at myself in the mirror. The stalking continued for a few months; luckily, I had my Earth Angel beside me, who picked me up from my lowest and darkest moments of my life and was there for me in every possible way.

Eventually the nightmare was evaporating when I got the police involved and was finally able to face him head on.

Game over.

But there was also one other person whom I needed to stop running from and stand up to, and that was myself. But I wasn't ready to face me yet.

Who am I anyway?

I began dating my Earth Angel—we both fell in love. Of course, considering my past, I questioned if his love was real. "How could anyone love me so much?" I thought. In my eyes I was so messed up, but through his eyes all he saw was a beautiful, strong, and loving woman who lit up his heart with happiness.

But I didn't see that within me.

Eventually, he adopted the father role in the relationship and I adopted the daughter role. Of course, this would eventually backfire in the intimacy department. I began to notice some resistance on his behalf and he too opened up to me about his fears with relationships. We became one another's counselor, thinking we could heal together. This didn't seem to be working and so I sabotaged the relationship.

I started dating other men and continued attracting the wrong ones.

One lonely night in my apartment, I was drinking and feeling miserable about my life. In that moment, I knew I was in a dark place. I crawled to the bathroom and did my business over the toilet bowl. Once finished, I looked into the mirror and into my eyes. For the first time, I felt I connected with my true self—this was my soul. I began to cry like a baby, and out aloud I said, "Dear God, if you are out there, please help me! I cannot do this to myself anymore. Please take me. I no longer want to be here."

Almost instantly, my crying stopped, I felt this peace and love run through my body and heard a powerful voice within me telling me to pick myself up, go to bed, and when I wake in the morning I was to pull myself together and change my life.

And so I did.

The moment I became ready and willing to hop back into the driver's seat of my life, the Universe supported me by opening doors that led me to the right people. I discovered Louise L. Hay, read every book I could get my hands on and became a self-love junkie. I chose to pursue the path of healing, forgiveness, self-discovery, and intensive self-love. I saw spiritual mentors, healers, psychologists, and life coaches who supported me toward paving my new road of peace, love, and happiness and making my self-care a priority.

As I connected the dots to my past, and reconnected with my childhood and relationship history, I became consciously aware and grasped the understanding of my life's decisions—I gained clarity and acceptance.

I went on a dating hiatus and, instead, dated myself. I took the time to heal and detox my life, and I became committed to my self-love journey. I re-discovered who I was at my very core and began to give the love that I denied from myself in the past when I was hoping a man could give it to me. I demonstrated acts of self-love by acknowledging myself for all the amazing qualities I had, which helped build my self-esteem.

Slowly, I became the love that I so desired to experience and discovered that I did not need to be in a relationship to be complete.

If you desire to create the love of your dreams, your first step is to date yourself. Spend some time to heal, detox your life, and learn to love yourself. The lover you attract will be your mirror, reflecting your best and worst.

About the Author

Irene Elias is a life coach, motivational speaker, and author. She delivers soulful life coaching for women ready to seduce themselves into becoming s.e.l.f l.o.v.e junkies to strengthen the relationship with themselves so they can create the love of their dreams and follow their heart's desires.

Irene is the author of the ebook *The S.e.l.f.L.o.v.e Junkie Guide: 8 Steps to Building the Life and Love of Your Dreams*.

http://www.ireneeliascoaching.com

WAITING FOR A MIRACLE

Jasmine Platt

"It's depressing news, I'm afraid. She probably won't walk—or talk. You probably won't ever know how she perceives the world. She will probably be just as she is now."

My mind went blank. The faces of the medical team were grim—their eyes fixated on me. Thirty seconds earlier, their careful pulling up of chairs to sit down had not felt like a good sign, not when ward rounds were usually standing, positively chirpy and at pace. Nor had the presence of six of them compared with the usual one.

Today was catastrophically different. This moment, I could tell, had just defined our future.

These ugly beige walls. Behind me, the beeping of heart monitors. Six sets of eyes studying my face, if not for recognition that I understood what they were saying, then to be ready to catch me if I passed out.

I felt dizzy and confused.

"What are they talking about?" I wondered. "What just happened? Am I awake? How do I wake up? Is this real?"

I looked down at my newborn lying motionless in her crib as they explained a condition where 50 percent die before age two—and the other 50 percent stay forever "vegetative".

I looked back at their faces. They all looked serious.

"This is actually happening," I realized.

My idyllic vision of watching our daughters happily playing and squealing together in the garden, spending summers at the beach and growing into happy, healthy young women: smashed. Replaced instead by a shattering vision and future of bedside vigil, counting seizures, administering medication, and cleaning her after bodily responses until either we or she died or until—a thought no more palatable to me—we put her into an institution for someone else to look after her.

Two months earlier, my life could not have been more different. I was the happiest person I knew. I loved my life and my career was sky-rocketing. As a personal and spiritual development trainer and coach, I was becoming known as "The Miracle Maker", training people how to turn their minds into "miracle machines".

And here we were, in need of a miracle beyond even my comprehension. I had no experience of this magnitude to go on—and my level of trust that things could be turned around was minuscule.

I could not comprehend the future they'd just told me to expect.

Each day, for five weeks as they tried to get our baby's seizures under control, there was nothing to do but sit for eighteen-plus hours a day, counting and recording the number and length of each and every seizure, calling for nurses—while struggling to confront our family's new reality.

Most people can't imagine a day spent sitting in the same chair doing nothing, let alone a day spent watching newborn seizures, let alone the thirty-five days we spent watching them in the hospital before being sent into the world to attempt to cope with it on our own.

During that time, one of the nurses became concerned—about me. Having silently watched as I became increasingly withdrawn, she ordered me to "get some fresh air".

Disoriented and confused, I wandered around—and found myself outside a hair salon.

The impeccable blonde hairdresser was chirpy and friendly. Typically hairdresserish.

I barely made it out without breaking down. But as soon as I got in the car, the screaming started. It started as incomprehensible, high-pitched yelling interspersed with struggling gasps and strange noises I'd never heard, coming from the depths of my heartbreak. Every part of me was breaking, and I couldn't keep it in any longer.

"Don't take my baby! How am I supposed to go on without her? Why—why is this happening?"

I shouldn't have been driving. The tears were coming so thick and fast, it was like driving through a rain-storm. But the grief was so heavy and deep, I didn't care. Finally coming to a stop in the middle of the next intersection, a man I almost collided with shook his fist at me. I couldn't have cared less if we'd crashed and killed us both.

That night was just the first of many to come of an absolute inability to cope.

I've always believed that life deals the hand and you play the cards—but I never expected to be dealt anything like this.

Over those weeks, they ran multiple drug tests—and then ran out of options. They tried steroids and a plethora of medications. Nothing worked.

There was nothing more they could do, except hope that her seizures would, at some point, become controllable. They had to discharge us to make way for a new child they could help. We would have to take her out into the big wide world with no one to be there if we needed them, no experience of what to do, and no reassurance about what was going to happen.

Sitting on the hallway floor of the ward as they were preparing to discharge us, having helped countless people create miracles in their lives, I thought if there was anyone who *should* be able to shift something, *it should be me*. But pulling off this kind of medical miracle? Doctors, the neurologists, many hours trawling Google—none could provide us any hope that a baby with her condition had ever had a future other than two equally catastrophic prognoses we'd been given.

With no option, I grabbed a pen and wrote a list I called "miracles in transit" that requested three unimaginable things. That:

1. Her seizures would stabilize

2. She comes off meds and be completely seizure-free

3. She develops normally.

My faith in any of them actually happening was, in all honesty, miniscule. I didn't believe things could get worse.

I was wrong.

A month later, Mylee was still having multiple seizures. Nothing had changed. No miracle delivered. After holding it together after months, I cracked.

I could no longer touch or hold her without having a full-blown panic attack. How could I be near her, my flesh and blood, knowing she may be taken from me?

I could feel myself at every moment, a hair's-breath from curling into a ball and screaming till there was nothing left.

Knowing I wasn't coping, my husband, my hero, became both "Mom" and "Dad". Watching him getting up multiple times through the night and leaving his work during the day to give her milk and medication, I felt wracked with guilt at being so unhelpful and useless, but I was paralyzed with gut-wrenching panic.

Each day, I spent most of the day on the couch, including eight slow, torturous hours of expressing breast-milk to give her some sustenance amongst her concoction of medication. Time stood still.

I didn't talk much—and anything I did say was negative. I barely moved off the couch. I lived off cups of tea. Mom called me "beige"— a nice way of saying I wasn't there anymore.

In desperation, my mom and husband staged an intervention, sending me to our doctor to try and "get me back".

On hearing that I had the worst depression score the doctor had ever seen, I accepted her recommendation to go on medication. The maternal mental health team she referred me to sent me to a post-natal depression therapy group. The other moms in the group were challenged by their baby's lack of schedule and how hard it was to have two kids in the bath at once. I was not among peers. They were lovely, but our realities were nothing alike.

Before I'd been pregnant with Mylee, I had written a "development plan"—a list of skills and qualities I wanted to practice and deepen. It included transforming my ability to be present, and to trust and surrender to a whole new level. I wanted to channel like the masters, and I knew trust, surrender, and presence were my access.

With no options left, I finally surrendered to the spiritual practices I had taught numerous clients for years.

Within days, Mylee started an unusual, new arm movement. One of the neurologists had warned us about an additional brain condition that could cause a different type of seizure that would start at around five months. In panic, we hurried to hospital for another scan.

For twenty-four hours, we waited anxiously, anticipating more bad news. If it was this new condition, the dark clouds were about to get blacker—if that was even possible.

When time came for the diagnosis, my heart was in my throat, my stomach contents ready to empty onto the floor.

The neurologist sat down. "I have looked at Mylee's EEG."

I searched her face for any sign.

"The scan shows nothing we wouldn't expect to see for a baby her age. It is normal." She smiled warmly. "Congratulations—she appears to be a miracle baby."

I sat with my husband in disbelief, waiting for an explanation, some hint of certainty that they hadn't read the wrong scan. And then hope started to creep in.

That was twenty-six months ago.

Mylee is now two and a half. She is still very much alive and is doing amazingly well.

The day of the spiritual practice I tried in desperation, Mylee had her final seizure. She came off anti-seizure medications several months later—and despite the original prognosis, with therapy, our miraculous wee girl is becoming increasingly mobile and verbal. Her full potential is still unknown, but my faith has now taken over.

I am often stopped by strangers to be told what an angel she is. She radiates love, light, and joy and connects with people in ways that move them in ways they don't understand.

It's been a road that has been challenging beyond description, but it is my absolute honor and privilege to be her mother. Her journey has broken me into tiny fragments and lovingly invited me to create myself anew.

My life before was a beautifully crafted painting. It is now a *mosaic of conscious choice*. I have kept the bits I wanted and have discarded the ones that no longer fit my vision for who I am or want to be.

I no longer experience fear in the little things, yet I am sensitive and vulnerable—compassionate and empathic in ways I could never access before. I am broken, weakened and strengthened, but at the same time, joyfully alive in my newfound comfort to call the present moment my home.

It's true that you get what you wish for but not necessarily in the way you expect. Trusting in the perfection of the journey can be damned hard at times. Two years on, while I wouldn't wish our journey on anybody, I also wouldn't change a thing.

Mylee has taught me love, trust, presence, patience, surrender, and joy.

May you, Dear Reader, always believe in the power of miracles to make your dreams come true.

I wish you the courage to ask faithfully for what you want and the patience to allow life to unfold in soulful and divine perfection.

While the path may not always go as you expect, I hope you choose to see beyond the uncertainty of grey skies or the bleakness of dark ones, trusting that while your dreams may not be within sight, they *are* within reach.

If life isn't going your way, trust that everything is always perfect—even when you can't see why—and have the patience to allow life's beautiful unfolding to reveal perfection and welcome your dreams.

I wish you immeasurable Love, Inspiration, and Miracles.

About the Author

Jasmine Platt is a highly-regarded miracle and happiness coach, trainer, and business mentor, whose take on life is that it's short and that we owe it to ourselves to love it—and to the world to do something worthy with it.

Jasmine writes on life, love, leadership, business, legacy and *all things happiness*. She is dedicating her life to helping others claim happiness, inspiration, and miracles in their lives for themselves.

http://www.jasmineplatt.com

BIRTHING THE SOUL

Andrew Nip

It was a bright summer afternoon, I laid softly on my arms resting on top of my desk. I had just ended a relationship that I truly thought would last for the rest of my life. Having given my heart away, there seemed to be no pieces left for myself. Nothing in this world mattered to me any longer. Somehow, my heart had led here. . . .

Sunken in a state of utter despair, I needed some answers. Little did I know that my questions . . . were going to completely transform my life.

I asked God. . . .

Why am I still alive?

What's the purpose of having such a big heart?

Why...?

And with that, I collapsed; all my thoughts and worries disappeared in an instant. I let go of everything that no longer had meaning, including my life.

Right then and there, I found myself floating in the sky, passing through the clouds, as an unknown force guided me forward. After a few short moments, a magnificent light, much like the sun's, appeared before me.

It was so overwhelmingly bright that I could not look at it directly, yet it was strange how it didn't hurt my eyes at all. Its color was so exquisite, resembling white mixed with tinges of gold, silver, and a fused coat of diamond. It beautifully shone a visual tone that does not exist in my world.

As I made a greater effort to look directly at the light, I caught a glimpse of its figure. There were these large wings spread out with a powerful grace. Upon seeing this, I instantly reawakened inside my room, with my jaw hanging in utter amazement, and was left with only a feeling that . . . I was *love*.

I quickly asked myself, *"What just happened?! It couldn't have been a dream, because I have never had a dream this real. Nor could it have been my imagination; my daydreams are never this real!!"*

And with that, my journey began . . .

The Catalyst

A few months had passed before I accidentally met a very strange fitness trainer. One of the first things he said to me was, *"It's no coincidence that you found me; there is a reason for everything."*

My first thought was this must be a new sales technique.

He combined meditation with his personalized workout programs. Along with affirmations, crystals, yoga, seeing auras; anything that you could think of that was out of the ordinary. Things that were out of the ordinary always fascinated me, as if life suddenly became filled with unlimited possibilities. It gave life a type of magic. So I just couldn't resist his program, as my inner child could not stop drooling!

After about two or three months of meditation, I experienced a breakthrough. It started off just like any other day. I was sitting on my mediation cushion almost half asleep due to fatigue, only this time near the end of the session I slipped into a whole new realm of reality.

I found myself merged with everything. Somehow, everything and nothing were the same thing. Time became non-existent or, better yet, the experience of time was a miniature point within the eternal space I was now in. Everything was *one*.

The closest words I could ever conjure to describe the experience is . . .

"Eternal Bliss"

Eternal because it is beyond time yet carries the nature of time.

Bliss because this is not a word many have experienced, one of utter fulfillment.

When I reawaked, immediately my not-so-quiet ego moaned, *"Oh, my God! This body is so heavy compared to where I just was; being in here, life is actually suffering!"*

It is true: the best moment in life—whether it is getting married or seeing a child being born—would still be a form of suffering in comparison. It is *that* powerful. It is a sense of fulfillment beyond all human understanding, of utter completion: a place where you go to and want to stay forever.

I thought to myself that if I could just enter this state a few seconds a day, I would always be happy no matter how difficult life was. This experience shattered all my previous beliefs about reality. I *know* now that deep down, we are all an expression of the eternal oneness.

Kundalini

As I turned twenty-two, I was about to walk into one of the toughest tests of my life. I went into what people called a "healing crisis", where my body did an extreme detox on its own; i.e., dumping away everything that was toxic.

Physically my lifelong devotion to fast food had backfired as my body detoxed through my skin, causing me to scratch open until I was bleeding every day. Emotionally, I carried so much anger and hatred as a child. I did not know I was a very sensitive kid: I felt what others were feeling and even took on their state, not knowing they were not of my own. The area I grew up in was filled with fear, violence, and anger. Quite often I heard gunshots and police sirens which were the music of my environment. This didn't help me very much nor did my family, who could have had their names placed in every dictionary underneath the word fear.

Looking back, it is apparent I was being *prepared*. Everything inside of me at all levels had to be cleared.

Some people called this period the dark night of the soul. Well, mine wasn't a night... Oh no, that would have been like a walk in the park.

Mine lasted for more than 365 days!!! In every single one of those days, death looked so much more pleasant than life. I was constantly in pain; I kept scratching myself, hoping to tear open so my blood would drain out. Thoughts about dying lured me—thousands of times—into ending the excruciating pain, which didn't seem to have an end.

Normally, a healing crisis is not supposed to last longer than a week for most people, but, as always, I was an extreme case. So my purification was more intense, my path tougher to walk, and friend were rare to find. I was all alone in the dark with only myself dripping in tears asking, "Why?"

What did I do wrong to deserve what I was getting? I really didn't know. . . .

I was like a caterpillar inside its pupa awaiting to be reborn.

Soul Longing

All of this passed, and I regained my health slowly. Now I was about to graduate from university, a pivotal point in everyone's life. As we ask ourselves the big question:

What am I going to do for a living?

I was still searching for the purpose of my life. A bright light with pretty wings didn't exactly answer my question. It did not say, *"Andrew, here is your sacred mission, You will pack your bags tomorrow, fly over to Tibet, climb a mountain, knock on a large wooden door, and the first bald man you see there will explain everything."*

Unfortunately, it didn't exactly turn out quite like that.

Frustrated, I walked over to a basketball court to let loose. To my surprise, there was no one there that day. Which is rare. I went on to dribble and shoot around hoping to let go of this tough question, but it just wouldn't let go of me! I REALLY needed to know!!!

Out of instinct I threw my basketball up as high as I could towards the sky and asked the universe, " *WHAT DID I COME HERE TO DO!?*" I caught the ball as if I was catching the answer. Again I threw it up requesting an answer. I did this three times before I walked home, still longing for an answer…

Within two to three business days, a friend spoke to me of her relationship issues. This was highly unusual as she has never opened up before. She spilled her guts, and as I listened in silence she spilled some more. Out of nowhere words came through me, and, without noticing how much time had passed, my friend was released of her troubles. I realized the advice I gave her was incredibly wise and loving. Just minutes ago she was locked under extreme depression and now she was completely freed, left with only a sense of joy and empowerment. What's even stranger was that I said to her, "I am going to become a writer."

Suddenly, it all clicked!

In the past, every time I spoke to a close friend about what we wanted to do for a living, a deeper part of me would flow out and say,

"I want to teach love."

But my mind would quickly jump in and rationalize: *"I don't have any gift that would allow me to accomplish such a huge task."* And so I left it aside . . . until *now*, when it showed up looking for me!

Magic

I remember since a young age that I could never see the sky clearly. I would always see lights swirling around, so I always thought I had an issue with my eyes. As I learned to see energy, the lights around me became clear. I saw thousands of sparks that swirled around me. Each made a half circle and left a white tail disappearing in a split second before another would appear. There would be a glow around my body as the more and more I let go of writing and allowed messages to flow through. Everything glowing and vibrating.

I don't know why I wrote. Every time my mind was still I would have a flood of information flowing through me as if someone was shouting, *"Andrew! This is important. You need to get this on paper."* What was going on? It was as if the quieter I got, the louder the messages became.

Because of my terrible English skills, thanks to an education that failed to keep me awake, I spent two years just picking up new words and sayings. I read books (an act that used to make me vomit) to help me convey the messages that kept flowing through me.

It had always been impossible to put anything meaningless inside my head. To me, English had always been meaningless. I hated using words to communicate messages, because they lack substance and depth. But now, I was driven again to transform from being something I was to something I was to become.

I don't know why, but it all *felt* right, somehow. I just knew that in this madness had meaning. . . .

So through these three years, I was turned from an undercover ESL student allergic to writing into someone who wrote in the car, bus, bed, and just about everywhere! I would have never dreamt, wished, nor planned for this to happen. But life is funny, as it just has its own plans when the heart leads the way.

All the life-transforming wisdom was flowing through me like a waterfall. I understood how we all can find true lasting happiness in every area of life: from finding Mr/Mrs. Right, having a peaceful family, to living your dream, to being enlightened and integrating that into the human experience.

The book is about to be completed while at least nine others are waiting to land on paper, each carrying the capacity to transform your life into the greatest experience beyond your wildest imagination. I'm here to help you live from your heart again and rediscover the beauty of the deepest truth lying within you waiting to be expressed into this world.

I started out a few years ago as a knucklehead who just wanted to know the purpose of my life. My questions took me to so many places. Through extreme pain to ultimate satisfaction, one thing is for certain: I got the answers to those questions.

And here is my secret
I knew it...
all along.

About the Author

Andrew Nip is an illuminating teacher who teaches you how to find real lasting love and happiness in your life. He sweeps away the barriers you have between you and what you really want, so that each and every part of your life reflects the vision of your soul. In his powerful presence, you will be lifted off your chairs and fast-forwarded towards your greatest joy. Whether it is your love life, family, work, or spiritual awakening, he sets you off towards what you desire with a passion that will transform worlds.

http://www.andrew-nip.com

WORTH IT

Stephanie Hamilton

"Wow, he sounds just like the Crocodile Hunter!" my mother squealed excitedly as the antiquated phone line crackled from the Saudi telephone connection.

"Um—yeah, Mom, he's actually from New Zealand. I think the Crocodile Hunter is from Australia, but they do sound a bit similar I guess!" I try to streamline things as the phone crackles again in my ear.

We are two souls, entwined in one cloud of ecstasy.

Canadian girl, 27, meets Kiwi boy, 26, in the middle of the desert: a vast sweeping land of dunes in the Empty Quarter of Saudi Arabia. We are surrounded by incredible beauty, wonderment, and soulful electricity.

It was exactly that electricity that entwined our souls to connect.

"I always knew I'd feel the thunderbolt," James would later proclaim at our wedding, "when you know, you know, and for me this was definitely a thunderbolt moment".

Thunderbolt, indeed.

Two weeks prior to this out-of-body moment and we were none the wiser. We didn't really even know the other existed, and yet, we were destined to remember. Two weeks before this encounter we had started the dance, but it took a trip to an ancient land, and stripping back nature's elements to recharge that electrical remembrance deep within our souls.

"Will you marry me?" he asked.

Our heart and soul is made of electrical impulses. We are pulsating vessels of light energy that vibrates to unique frequencies, and it was this unique energy that was grounded in the desert sand that day. Beautiful light poured into our crown through the power of the sun and brought us back to our knowingness of love.

But, of course, love has its own agenda, and it's not the version you've been told in the tales of Cinderella or Sleeping Beauty.

No, it's a much deeper and a more complex rite of passage that takes us through the highs and lows and brings us to the great understanding of our power.

Hallmark will tell you otherwise, as will the likes of every romantic based corporation that thrives on the creation of tales similar to that which I've shared with you. Our culture has thrived on the creation of romanticism, the small details, and moments that take your breath away. That's what sells, but it's not the entire story!

Our wedding was an event like no other. People flew to Canada from all over the world. It was like the United Nations of weddings!

Two weeks of knowing each other, and we were engaged. It was the news of the year; in fact, it was the news of the century as we had just passed into the millennium!

There was a line in the celebrant's speech that said something to the effect of "Boy from New Zealand meets girl from Canada in the middle of the desert in Saudi Arabia. If you look at the map you could say that they met each other halfway." The irony in that statement is comical in that this is a primary theme in our relationship!

Fast forward six years. I've just given birth to my second daughter, Ruby. Ruby has Down Syndrome, and as I loved her deeply from the first moment I saw her and felt a sense of protection for this beautiful and vulnerable being, I also felt a deep aching within the chasm of my soul. An aching for a feeling of completion, connection and a search for perfection. In those moments, the ache was dull, and the pain suppressed. My ego would not allow for such a rash display of emotions at that time.

I smile, proclaim that this is our destiny, and march on in the echo of the emptiness of my soul. And looking back, this is what I suspect James did too.

This was the defining moment that my soulful connection with my husband began to shift. This is not the type of thing you're supposed to admit or that you're supposed to write about, knowing that millions of people are about to read it.

But it's true.

From that point on, I had never felt so much love, and yet I had never felt so many moments of loneliness.

And before I carry on, it's important to emphasize that Ruby's entry into our soul plan was always fully accepted. We both knew, deep down, that this was meant to be. It was always written that she chose us, and we chose her.

There was never a point of rejecting her, and we always have embraced the challenge of being her parents, fully and unconditionally.

That's not to say that it hasn't come at a price. That's not to say that love doesn't come in many forms and that, in this case, love presents itself as the challenge of how we function as her parents, yet keeps the dream alive within our relationship.

The loneliness and separation I have felt in our relationship as we both navigate our own pathways through not only being a parent to Ruby, but also to our two other daughters goes beyond what I've ever imagined it to be.

Of course, the question arises: how am I a reflection of this loneliness that I feel? Am I not my own person, and am I not surrounded by beautiful and supportive people? And yet, I feel isolated and alone.

To be a part of a flame, whether it be the inner strength and peace of the blue in the belly of the fire or the gold that rises boldly above it, is to navigate the dance of danger.

To maintain the integrity of the dance of the flame, to savor its passion, to create the warmth and union it provides, and to not get burned, is the ultimate test of love.

To dodge the effigies of blame, hurt, rejection, loneliness, victimhood, and desperation requires great skill. Isn't this what love primes us for? Isn't this how we prepare to savor the beauty of the flame when it burns clean?

When all the residues of our challenges have been engulfed and clarified, our emotions stand justified and we rise from the ashes with a deeper connection than we ever knew was possible.

It was not until quite a few years after Ruby was born that James was able to truly express the feelings that were pent up inside him and that I was able to see the beauty of how we chose this path together: how that path was clearly signposted with "LOVE". We had been struggling in our relationship and even questioning if we were meant to be together at this point. Sometimes, it can all seem so overwhelming, especially when everyone around you wears the mask of perfection and is too afraid to share their cracked existence.

But then you realize that in the cracks, lies a deeper layer far beneath. This layer is fresh, and when exposed, provides infinite possibilities for renewal in that existence.

And so, the dance continues, in perfect unison and fluidity. The souls remember, forgive, and unite once again. Those times when things were rough, when we retreated back into ourselves, were necessary.

The loneliness is what feeds the vessel of love. It creates a yearning which manifests into many other channels until it's able to resurface in perfect harmony.

We are sold the dream of perfect harmony. In all the relationships I've been exposed to, I believe that perfect harmony exists in the pain, and the resurfacing and survival of that pain. There is no magic bullet, no field of poppies to mask the truth of why we come into one another's lives.

The truth provides us with an open vista of glorious meadows, dark and tainting forests, treacherous climbs, and smooth sailing in our relationships.

It has been through my soulful connection to my soul mate James that I have experienced each and every one of these vistas. Pain has been the fuel that has created a deeper connection of understanding and compassion.

It's not always easy for me to understand why my life doesn't resemble a Hallmark card, and yet, strangely, I quite like the beautiful mess of reality that I live in.

In fact, it is down to gratitude that I feel the greatest connection back to myself, which I can then reflect back through my relationships. I have always considered myself a thankful person, but as a human being, it is natural to take things for granted.

It has been in the darkest moments of feeling disconnected to myself, to my husband, and to my children that I have sought refuge in the arms of nature. I have picked up a camera, walked out the front door, and discovered a whole structure of support surrounding me with an overwhelming sense of love and acceptance. It was through this profound reconnection with nature, that I was able to restore the balance within myself.

Feet firmly planted on the ground, and I can feel again. Head filled with the warmth of the glorious sun, and I am filled with purpose. Wind in my hair, and a chill down my spine, and I feel the strength of my being. Rain on my face, and I know that I am vulnerable, yet provided for.

In those moments of misunderstanding in our relationship, an exercise of strength, will, and purpose has provided the means for us to grow. After all, love is a muscle. It needs exercise and care like any other part of us. The more you engage in the challenge, the stronger the muscle becomes.

"So you're saying love is a muscle?" I hear you ask.

You heard me right. But here's the thing: sometimes you need to crack the exterior to get to the softness inside. A broken heart, split in every direction, allows the lava to flow—to envelope our soul in the knowingness that love is real, love is raw, and yes, love requires an element of pain.

To exercise the muscle of love, to allow it to contract and expand, and to burn and be soothed is the purity of truth and wholeness in a relationship.

James and I have been through many, many challenges, including huge overseas moves, job losses, family issues, depression, and the trials of parenting a child with special needs.

The disconnection that occurs in these times of challenge is essential to allow the love to grow and to see things from a greater perspective. We have experienced intense, passionate connections with one another, but we have also lived under the same roof, connected by the finest thread that is the remembrance of our soul connection, which has allowed us the space to navigate the next level of our relationship.

I wouldn't and couldn't even begin to sugar coat things. That powerful union we had in the desert, it was meant to be, and continues to be, a driving force in our relationship. The stuff in between, it has been raw, real, joyful, blissful, painful, passionate, ecstatic, and heartbreaking.

There are plenty of Tiffany & Co boxes up in my wardrobe, there is also a substantial diamond ring that was chosen and pondered over back in that Saudi desert over thirteen years ago. There are trips to the Maldives, weekend getaways, and beautiful dinners fit for a queen. These things are beautiful, memorable, even breathtaking, yet there is nothing that compares to the beauty of wading through that deep river or climbing that treacherous peak to reveal the softness that lies within the entwinement of our souls. To carry the load for one another in those moments of disconnection is bittersweet, but it is the essence of the truth, of both the struggle and the triumph.

And it is worth it; oh, yes, it is *worth* every single lonely, heartbreaking, and beautiful moment that has ever been endured to know that the sweetness of spirit lies within, waiting to connect and to understand that the journey was more important than the destination, and that destination is love.

About the Author

Stephanie Hamilton has lived as an expat for the past seventeen years. Mother of three, and the Creative Visionary behind her brand Nektar, she is a published author, soul photographer, and Spiritual and Life Alignment Coach. Stephanie is also an Aura-Soma® Color Practitioner, having had great success with her Soulmap program using the energies to color, sound, and vibrational energy to help her clients unlock their true soul blueprint and magnificence. Stephanie is active in creating awareness for equality and inclusion in society through the stories of children with Special Needs. Stephanie has supported several charities through her businesses including AAO in Sierra Leone and Lifestart Foundation in Vietnam.

http://www.nektar.ae

BEAUTIFUL JOURNEY, LIVING WITH SOUL

Helen White

In all relationships, what is created by the act of "relating" is a space between two entities: a shared void of creative interchange that somehow amounts to more than the sum of its parts. When that relationship is with the soul, or Higher Self, it allows for the drawing down of that unharried multi-perspective and overview that our eternal version has to offer.

Our soul is not something external, I now realize; it is simply a non-physical version of Self that can only come to know itself by putting its physical counterpart, our human form, through the contorted perspectives provided by what I often refer to as "theme park Earth". Connection with the soul remains like a door left ajar when we are children; yet, as beliefs start to be ingrained, imitated, and strategically adopted in the name of survival, the voice of Higher Self is often considered far too abstract to listen to—heeded only in rarest moments of acute intuition or creativity.

When we cease the open dialog with Higher Self, of course, that soul steps in with other modes of communication, nudging us through experience after experience to get us back into alignment—something that can be done the easy way or, when we are in resistance, the long and arduous one.

As a deeply intuitive, sensitive, and creative child preferring my own company, I remained attuned to soul-voice for an idyllically extended time until, as a teenager, the new voice of self judgement started to shout it down.

By my twenties, I had developed a profound fear of self-expression, in spite of having much to say. I had also internalized the belief that the aim of life was to "partner up" and, despite all signs to the contrary, took the contorted view that I was uniquely unattractive, peculiar, and unlovable. In both personal and professional domains, I was held rigid by a fear that, if I stepped out, I would be ridiculed, rejected, or silenced; for these can be potent fear patterns embedded from many lifetimes.

Invisibility seemed to be my only haven, yet this locked me into an impasse with opposing desires to be seen and heard. From the soul perspective, it was clear that I needed to travel through the very thick of these skewed perspectives—so experiencing them fully in all of their distortion—before I could find my way back to my bliss and myself.

To achieve this, I manifested a thirteen-year relationship that felt so wrong and yet gripped onto, in that way we have of perpetuating those "stuck" patterns that serve some soul-purpose beyond our limited perspective. This relationship had a perfection all of its own because it exposed me to my very worst fears about myself through a steady flow of put-downs and treatment that left me demeaned, desperate to please and to keep the peace.

Bravest moments of self-expression were quashed with comments that provided self-sought "evidence" that I had made a fool of myself or that I was not liked. My appearance was never good enough—always something to be worked on. Creativity was shrivelled down to the level of home-maker skills, whilst all the loving attention I had long-since withheld from myself was poured into the pseudo-parent role that I took on as a wife: one which collided head on with my actual role as a parent after my daughter was born.

In dismay, I watched as my one loving ally, my mother, succumbed to cancer within eight months of diagnosis. My life had become the very mirror of my worst fears, and I felt utterly forsaken.

On the contrary, Higher Self was still being the best friend that I had. At some point, I must have heard it cry "enough" because, catalyzed by the love of my daughter where love of myself had failed, I turned to face the fear head on: I divorced.

Now alone with a young child, facing bankruptcy and juggling two stressful jobs, there was nothing to be done but to keep wading through the mire until I reached what felt like moderately firmer footing on the other side. That was the moment when my health collapsed. Almost overnight, I witnessed my body dissolve under a myriad of physical symptoms, including chronic pain and over-whelming fatigue; and no wonder—I had been squirreling away emotional pain for years and its manifestation in the physical body was simply Higher Self's way of announcing this!

It was around that time that, just as life had come to feel like a col-lection of painful memories stuffed into a cupboard, a literal cup-board of junk revealed a box of oil paints that had, ironically, been a rare gift from my ex husband. Drawn to try them, the first thing I experienced through painting was a temporary respite from pain, then a sort of ease and flow combined with an indefinable quality akin to profound joyfulness or bliss.

Painting took me into a kind of meditation, and this became a regu-lar meeting ground with Higher Self. As I painted what came out of these meetings, inspiration poured in; at first, it was as though I was some sort of conduit for an entity outside of myself, but then I real-ized that this was me, from a place of no pain, fear, or duality. Just as I learned, through my brushstrokes, that it is impossible to paint light without dark—not the fear-based dark I used to imagine, but the quality that gives light something to push against, to contrast with—so I began to grasp the same thing about life.

As I got the feel of my creator powers within the bounds of a canvas, I detected parallels with all that was happening in the bigger picture, became newly inspired to experiment with how my actions create my reality, and so gained a tangible sense of the I Am: the manifes-tor that had been there all along. Just as all the multifragmented color I loved to depict in my paintings seemed to mirror the new ease with which I was starting to celebrate the sheer diversity and experiential "soup" that make up life itself, I found that the new place of stillness that I was learning to hold intact within myself, regardless of life's ups and downs, was mirrored by an ever-growing fascination with what I now regard to be my core subject: the full-spectrum all-that-isness that is light.

As with all relationships, once rapport is established—even in short bursts—there is less need for those other experiential attention-grabbers that dive in from left field, so life's dramas begin to sub-side. Meditation and a whole new journey into expanded conscious-ness have moved this communication along for me, and, although I still have moments of lapse or bewilderment, I am getting so much better at stepping back from *whatever* unfolds to consider "What's wrapped-up in this? What is Higher Self showing me that I can process by having this experience?"

When I lived from a place of fear, even a minor downturn of events could floor me; I had come to regard fear as a literal "stop" sign.

Now, when things happen that I do not like, even those which are real ground-shakers, I no longer hold them in my body but, remaining grounded, allow their energy to pass through me with considerably more ease than before. The viewpoint that no circumstance is intrinsically "bad" has transformed my experience of life and, going backwards, has enabled me to reconcile what I have been through in such a way that I have unearthed gifts in the darkest of corners—like those paints falling out of the cupboard. One of the most profound has been the remembrance that life is meant to be playful, easy, and fun and that there is no mission, nothing that I "have" to do, no one that I need to "save".

With ever-increasing confidence, I have found that the integration of such a viewpoint into my experience has turned my health right around from where it was five years ago and left me ready to declare, without apology, that life is joyful.

Being, as it were, the archetype of all relationships, the one we have with our soul uses the mirror of our world to communicate with us, and so we can be sure that the relationships we have with everyone else, from our spouse (I now have a loving and supportive one of *those*) to the girl behind the shop counter, are a reflection of that most significant of relationships at our core. Higher Self seeks to guide us back to its own full-spectrum perspective by enabling us to explore our way through a myriad of experiences until we become adept at sensing that we are getting ever closer to our bliss; yes, even when taken across the roughest terrain to get there.

Allowing this apparent paradox enabled me to release all the energy of regret and self judgement that had been stored within the fibres of my body and so embark on my healing journey in earnest. With this one puzzle-piece, I was able to grasp that there were no grudges to be held, no outcomes to be feared; everything had been played out, and would continue to play out, as a well-timed dance across a crowded floor filled with many others with whom we have prearranged contracts to cross paths and interact.

Seen from this perspective, all relationships *are* soulful-relationships, and this understanding has flooded me with newfound clarity and an untold amount of gratitude.

With this clarity, I appreciate how Higher Self has led me from that place of feeling so very stifled to where I am now openly communicating through paint and words, unfettered and flowing. From this place of flow, I have learned to experience the universe as an energy matrix and this has transformed all kinds of relationships, both personal and professional. Being open and expansive in my interactions, I find that the mirror of life reflects a very different reality to the one I knew before. Serendipitous connections occur all the time; chance encounters blossom into meaningful business relationships; and friendships of the heart occur across thousands of miles as I open myself wide in social arenas that used to terrify.

When I tried so hard to make my art commercial, selling my work was a struggle. Now that my art is only ever soul-inspired, I set an open-ended intention then sit back and watch as stories of extraordinary coincidence take shape amidst the supposedly random circumstances that dictate how each painting finds its owner, often left with the sense that I have been working to divine commission. As my intention has evolved beyond a mere depiction of light towards the incorporation of the very *energy* of light into my paintings, this has drawn ever more people to my work at a level of resonance that defies commercial stereotype.

The ability to incorporate energy into art is a profound gift from my soul. It enables me to interact with every other being who comes into contact with my work and to ripple that feeling out through them and beyond in a way that feels like the ultimate soulful-relationship of all—the one in which we all play a part as the collective consciousness that is source = sun = *light*. I am literally scattering light!

Looking back one last time, I see that the ultimate gift from Higher Self is the realization that I am ready to let go of this story; that through consciously creative eyes, I have achieved the full integration of the journey's ups and downs and previously-perceived battle scars into one perfect whole (that is as expansive as it is beautiful) and so this story is no longer required except in so far as it may help others through the sharing of it.

I hereby release it from my energy, scattering it to the wind.

About the Author

Helen White is a self-taught professional artist whose work is exhibited in galleries across the UK and beyond, including London and New York, as well as being held in private collections internationally. Her paintings of moments of light have been said to contain an energy all of their own and to seem like a portal into another dimension.

Her self-managed recovery from fibromyalgia and the profound connections that she perceived between creativity, expanded-consciousness, energy-awareness and balanced health led to the creation of a blog* which has added a growing readership to those who already follow her art work.

http://www.helenwhite.org
http://www.scatteringthelight.com

STEFANIE: MY CHILD AND SPIRITUAL GUIDE

Patricia Hung

For my birthday, after our second adoption, my husband, James, gave me a personalized licence plate that read *PIGEES*. Yes, both he and I are police officers, and, as amusing as that might be, each letter actually represents one of the names of our children: Patrick, Ian, Grace, Eric, Elena and Stefanie—although not in the correct birth order.

Stefanie and Ian are the biological children of my first marriage; Eric and Patrick of my second; and Grace and Elena, both born in our hearts, were adopted from China in 2009 and 2011 respectively.

On January 1, 2008, when Stefanie was fourteen years old, two disturbed individuals killed her. They are now both serving life sentences for first degree murder.

A seventeen-year-old boy, under pressure from his fifteen-year-old girlfriend to kill Stefanie, lured my daughter out of our home and stabbed her six times. She did her best to make it back to safety but collapsed in a snow bank in the icy-cold just feet from our driveway and succumbed to her wounds. She was alone and in terrible pain. We were just minutes from arriving home after having been out for dinner, but, when we got there, it was too late: she was already dead.

There are no words to describe how it feels when a child dies. Just as words are inadequate to accurately express the love we feel for our children, they fail as miserably to convey the pain we experience when they die. Who could ever fathom that someone would want to murder, literally, one of my children?

I wondered if I would ever experience real happiness again. Would that be possible, and if I ever managed such a feat, how could I live with the guilt of being happy when my daughter had suffered so much and then died before her life had hardly begun?

Aside from the emotional heartbreak after such a tragedy, there are so many other ensuing challenges—a loss of privacy during the police investigation, invasive media, trials, sentence hearings, and appeals. It never ends, it seems. As one finishes, there's another around the corner.

We all lost our sense of personal security and safety, especially Ian and me. I had horrible panic attacks when our other children were not at my side and lived in a constant state of fear, waiting for and expecting more bad news. As I was just holding on by the thinnest of threads, I feared any little incident would be my undoing.

Sadly, this has been our reality and the last five years have been a true test of faith and love as we've picked up the pieces of our broken lives and found hope again.

Witnessing the journey of Stefanie's siblings has been both heart-breaking and endearing. Ian was 12 at the time and was, suddenly, unable to relate to his peers, unsure of who to trust, and reluctant to leave the house.

Eric, who was five, had horrible night terrors and panicked any time Ian was away from home. He now knew that true evil existed—something a five-year-old should never have to face.

As Ian's fourteenth birthday approached, Eric was distraught. He was terrified that Ian might die like his sister had at fourteen—worried about himself when he reached that fateful age. That evening, while tucking Eric into bed, his fear palpable, I did my best to reassure him by reminding him that he was inside the house, that the doors were locked, and that we loved him and would never let anything happen to him. In his beautiful innocence and not realizing how his words would tear me apart, he asked me if I hadn't loved Stefanie enough to keep her safe.

Moments like these would knock me off balance and leave me gripping for the fragile stability I had moments before. Maintaining a secure and loving home life for the other children was paramount, and, although at times it made life so much more difficult, coupling their grief with ours, it also gave us a purpose for living.

Immediately, after Stefanie's death, I searched online and in books for any kind of comfort, something to speak to me directly—evidence that another mother in my situation had survived the murder of her first born, but my search came up empty. I vowed that if I was ever able to, I would take on that responsibility: to reassure someone as desperate as I was that it was possible not only to overcome strong suicidal feelings and survive, but also to fight through the pain to a life once more filled with joy.

As I found myself sitting in the aisles of my local bookstore, devouring anything I could get my hands on, frantic for answers, through tears of desperation, I asked for guidance. I had lost all my faith and couldn't stand on my own because the foundation under my feet had cracked and had fallen away.

The answer came in the form of a new friend standing at the top of a snowy hill in the blistering cold. We first met a few months before. Looking back at the seemingly insurmountable sequence of events that needed to occur for us to meet was incredible, and yet there we were. She, knowing nothing of my daughter's homicide, started to talk to me about the Law of Attraction. This was something completely new to me. Instinctively, I knew I had to learn more.

The Law of Attraction is the belief that we attract things and circumstances into our lives that correspond with both our conscious and subconscious thoughts and beliefs. We are all pure energy—body and mind—vibrating at different frequencies. The basic premise is that like energy attracts like energy, so we attract into our lives anything with which we are a vibrational match—good or bad. This happens because we are already connected to everything energetically, but we are physically unaware of this due to the limitations of our five senses when interpreting energy fields. The trick is to become a vibrational match to what we need and desire by making it our dominant frequency, and we need to change our thoughts and beliefs if we're going to change our dominant frequency.

I was both intrigued and horrified. On the one hand, it made utter and complete sense, yet, at the same time, it seemed impossible. Did Stefanie attract this into her own life? I needed to know more and wondered why I hadn't, in all the books I read about God and about spirituality and healing, come across these teachings. Sitting in that bookstore, I clearly wasn't ready, but at the top of that hill, as the cold seeped into my bones, I felt a warmth and a glimmer of hope for true healing and was inspired to learn all there was to know.

I had been so angry at God and didn't want to hear mention of His name. Therefore it was easy to use different terminology and substitute the idea of God for the idea of being part of a Universal mind from which all things manifest. This allowed me to safely rebuild my faith in something greater than myself. It didn't take long to realize that one is not mutually exclusive of the other, regardless of the label. God is not defined by one religious denomination or another, God *is* the Universal mind full of love and abundant joy. Each of us is connected to, and part of, this divine source of eternal love.

There is a kind of shattering that happens with the death of a child, particularly if it's a violent death. Aside from a heart left in a million pieces, you lose a sense of who you really are and what life is all about. The question "Why?" is the only one that matters then.

What's interesting is that once a life is crushed to that extent, the only thing left to do is rebuild a sort of emotional reconstruction. This is where we must face our darkest emotions and allow them to flow freely without any resistance and face them fully even if they hurt more than anything we've ever experienced. But surrendering fully eventually brings us to acceptance, and that's what brings gifts of wisdom, courage, and heightened compassion. We must stop resisting, thereby allowing the joy we desire to find a way to manifest itself in our lives.

Grief is a teacher, albeit an unwanted one, but once its gifts have blessed our lives, we are then freer to feel joy, love, and gratitude.

One of the biggest challenges was learning to be in a place of gratitude. I was so devastated by the death of my daughter that I would have easily given up anything I had to have her back. Practicing gratitude, privately and as a family, was the key to becoming more aligned with the joy we had once felt.

The children have all become incredibly heart-centered people. They are full of compassion and empathy for others, way beyond their years. Their growth has doubled mine. I find myself thanking Stefanie frequently, not just for the beautiful person she was, but for the gifts she has brought to our lives through her untimely and tragic death.

In order to attract joy, we must be courageous enough to open up a channel for those energies to flow toward us and through us to others. Giving thanks opened up small windows of serenity, allowing similar and more powerful positive energies to join us. Our positive thoughts brought about positive manifestations and continue to do so. When we have gratitude and courage as our building partners, we have a good chance at reconstructing a healthy, fulfilling life.

I know I can't bring my daughter back. But I am so grateful for all she has taught me and continues to teach me.

Before we are born, there is a plan for us in this life regardless of whether we choose it or not. I believe that I chose this difficult road to learn and grow but also to help others heal. Had my beloved daughter and I both been in heaven before coming to Earth and been asked who would like to help others ease their suffering, I would have stepped forward.

When asked who would teach me, she would have volunteered.

About the Author

Patricia Hung is a police officer, certified From Heartbreak to Happiness® coach, author, and sought-after keynote speaker. She is on numerous Victim Witness Advisory Committees.

Patricia is the director of performance coaching and delivery at ITC Greatness Performance Coaching Inc., and the owner of Coaching Joy which specializes in one-on-one grief coaching.

Patricia is also the mother of a murdered teenaged daughter.

Her work has been published in Canadian Family Magazine. She is the author of *Seven Helpful Ways to Support Those Who Grieve* and writes a blog.

http://www.joyintheaftermath.com
http://www.patriciahung.com

THREE TIMES A CHARM

Scott Bull

The story I am about to share with you is deeply personal and lays bare the depths of my soul. It is more than I have shared with anyone other than the love of my life, my beautiful wife. However, I feel that it is important to peel back the layers and to reveal my inner nature for the sake of what I believe to be true. I am not a relationship guru, not by a long shot. I've made my share of mistakes along the way. Do I believe in the ability to manifest soulful relationships?

Absolutely.

My story may seem to have all the elements for a Greek tragedy, yet I can assure you that it is very much a tale of modern life. Is it outside the realms of normalcy? Possibly; but it is my story.

Well, here I go. It all started when I was three years old. My father was killed in a light aircraft accident. A year later, my mother, a loving woman who felt she owed it to her children to give them a father, entered a relationship with another man. She had four children and so did he. You could say we were the archetypal "Brady Bunch". Unfortunately, my mother's choice did not turn out to be the best one for any of us as he was an abusive and violent alcoholic. To her credit, my mother remained married to him for thirty-six years, which included her making two suicide attempts. For his part, he tried to give up drinking, and for about the last ten years of their marriage, he was mostly successful.

I didn't have, what I later learned to be, a role model for a normal adult relationship, and this scarred my emotional development. One of my great desires throughout my childhood was that one day, when I married, I would not be like my parents. I would be "better". Famous last words, right? Well I thought so too for a long time.

At twelve years of age, I had had enough of my home environment and I left home voluntarily. I still had to go to school and so I finished schooling at boarding schools and state-run high schools. Oh, and don't think that my mother paid the school fees. I paid them out of the small amount of money left to me by my natural father.

At seventeen, I joined the police and at nineteen was a sworn police officer attending violent domestic disputes. All the while, I was consciously and subconsciously thinking that there had to be better relationships than these in the world. These people were damaging themselves and their children and making generational emotional cripples. I had a burning desire to be a father but didn't want to burden my children with my own baggage. Yet it was one of the basic drives that I felt I needed to fulfill.

Then I met someone. A beautiful young woman who liked me. We dated. We got engaged. She went on a cruise without me in the company of her best friend. When she came back, she told me of a shipboard romance. I transferred away, twelve hundred kilometers away, and broke off the engagement. Some months later she turned up on my doorstep with a used one-way plane ticket, a suitcase full of her worldly possessions and $100 to her name in the bank—not enough to get her back home to her parents.

I let her stay until she could afford to return home. Mistake number one. Two years later, we were married. Two years after that, I was away on a remote community at the tip of Cape York in Queensland, working in the police and earning money to pay off our mortgage. I had the opportunity to go home for the weekend, and I took it. Mistake number two. I found her naked in the arms of her boss, who until then was also one of my best friends. We divorced and I lost everything.

Two years later, I was again living with a wonderful woman who seemed to be everything I wanted. We planned to get married, build a house, and have kids. Yes! I thought I had finally beaten the curse of my upbringing. We married, bought land, built a house, and settled into our careers. Time passed and we didn't talk much about kids other than to say, "Yes. One day. Just not yet. Not now. Soon." Turns out, she didn't really want any children and was waiting for me to agree to not having any. I couldn't do that, and so she told me, "I don't want children. If you want children, then go find someone to have them with." I left, we divorced; and again I lost everything.

I was now emotionally devastated. Two attempts at marriage and two failures. I thought I was completely incapable of establishing a meaningful relationship. I felt that I would never have any type of deep, lasting love. I couldn't believe that the Universe was so cruel. How could it let me down this way when all I wanted was that deep soulful connection that you read about and see at the movies and on television? Where is that perfect soul? The other half of my soul mind, my twin flame. I truly believed that she was out there. I just had to find her.

I was still in the police during the period of my second separation and pending divorce. I was a mentor and training officer for new police fresh from the academy and needed to be on my game, enthusiastic and ready to catch them when they inevitably stumbled through putting their training into action. I was not in a good place to do that. So, when I separated from my second wife I was put in the watch-house, or the police cells as they may be known where you are from, so that I could take some time to gather myself emotionally.

While I was in the watch-house, I met a young female police trainee who made my heart pound, my breath catch in my throat, and caused me to blush when I looked at her. What was going on? I felt like an awkward teenager. She's married, I kept telling myself. Yes, she was married, happily married—or so I thought. Turns out that she was indeed happily married: her husband was happy and she was married.

About a year after we met in the watch-house, and after working together on and off on shift, I learned that she was separated from her husband. She was living with friends and, crushingly, was being kept away from her children, a girl and a boy. We spoke about our pain, and in one conversation she said that my last wife was stupid and she said, "I can see you would be a good father. I'd have your children." We moved on from that conversation as much closer friends.

In the police, we had an unofficial social club for divorcees and people going through separations. It was jokingly called the "bitter and twisted club". I was part of this club, and, now, so was this woman who continued to hold my attention. As a group, we would all go out regularly on social outings to restaurants and nightclubs. We were all damaged individuals, relationship shy, and definitely had no intentions of forming serious long-term relationships. Ha! The Universe had other plans for me. I still harbored the desire to be a father and this was to lead to something amazing.

That young woman, the one I met in the watch-house, still held my fascination and fired my imagination. I was like a deer in the headlights of an oncoming truck. I knew if I didn't move, I was going to be swept away. And that is exactly what happened.

We were working together one evening some time after we had become good friends and members of the "bitter and twisted club". We were checking our vehicle for damage prior to taking it out on patrol, and as we reached the trunk of the car, we both reached for the latch. Our hands were about an inch apart and zap. A static spark, plainly visible in the late afternoon light, jumped between our hands. We looked at each other in that instant. I nearly drowned in the twin pools of her eyes. I could see into her soul, and I knew this was her: the woman I had been waiting for my entire life. We both leaned in as if to kiss and then we realized where we were and who might be watching: our other police colleagues. It must have only been a few seconds, but it seemed like an eternity that we stood there looking at each other not wanting the moment to pass.

From that day on, we grew closer. We acknowledged our desire for each other and we moved in together. As all couples do, we made plans for our future. We struggled with our own demons and, yet, we supported each other without question or effort. It was the simplest of things to do, being there for each other.

Then, a miracle occurred. My soul mate, the woman I was living with, asked me if I was ready to be a father. My joy was boundless, yet so was my fear. I revealed my own damaged childhood and my fears that, despite my desire to be otherwise, I would end up being unable to provide a good role model for any children I might have.

There it was: the fear that had lain in wait for me all these years. My soul mate took me in her arms and looked me in the eyes and said, "You won't make those mistakes. You will be a good father. I know it in my heart and I can see it in your soul. I already have two children and I wouldn't make this offer without the certainty that you will be the best father I could give to my children and ours." Yes, she had said "ours". With that, the decision was made. My soul mate believed in me, so I now had the confidence to join with her in creating life. Nine months later, our first child was born, a son. A beautiful, healthy boy. My childhood desire, one of the basic drives of my life, had been fulfilled. Three years later, we were blessed with another young life to nurture. Another beautiful, healthy boy.

My third wife, and soul mate, and I met seventeen years ago. In that time, we have experienced the miraculous joy of creating new life. We have the two boys I have spoken of, and I have helped raise a daughter and a son from my wife's first marriage. We have grown together and become closer than I could possibly have imagined was achievable. We are raising a family free from the demons that haunted our early lives. We are wealthy, not in financial terms, but in the blessings of love and family that the Universe has entrusted us with.

The last seventeen years have been an adventure. One that continues to develop with each passing moment and one that I know in my heart will keep building in joy and happiness into a far distant future. I share this with you now as one story among many that make up this book. I do this so that you know, no matter who you are or where you find yourself emotionally, there is someone for everyone. Don't give up. Concentrate, focus your energies, and believe with all your heart that you will find that soulful connection—that twin flame, and it will come to pass for you as well.

Do I believe in the ability to manifest soulful relationships?

Absolutely!

About the Author

Scott Bull is on a journey of discovery. He writes for his own website and calls himself a spiritual warrior and seeker of the way. He writes about the things he unearths on his journey. These enlightening encounters cover a variety of topics for readers to contemplate in the quieter times of their lives. Scott also writes fiction.

For more of Scott's writings, visit his website.

http://www.timberwolfhq.com/

FALL IN LOVE WITH YOURSELF FIRST

Carly Evans

The day I began writing this chapter, I saw the quote "Don't forget to fall in love with yourself first" by Carrie Bradshaw. In one sentence, this summarizes what you're about to read. And yet it's something I've only learned in the last couple of years as being *the* most important soulful relationship you can have.

A couple years ago I found myself in the midst of *the black dog*—a smoky haze of depression. While I had moved from London to Australia just a year before, a dream I had for around ten years, here I was, wishing every day I woke up that I hadn't. Each day a friend of mine would call me and give simple instructions to follow.

"Sit upright in bed and then call me." So I did.

"Fling your legs over the side of the bed and then call me." So I did.

"Eat something then call me." And so I did.

I'd follow her instructions through simple tasks like having a shower and going for a walk—things I knew I should be doing to feel better but struggled to do without encouragement. I'll always be grateful to her for helping me at a time when my family and closest friends were a twenty-four-hour plane ride away.

Before I experienced depression for myself, I could have written a thesis on what "it" was: definitions of the different types, symptoms, environmental and physiological causes, as well as suggested treatments. I'd studied psychology since I was seventeen and did my Bachelor of Science and Masters in it. I'd worked for four years as a probation officer in London, and some probationers I worked with had major depression. A little over a year before my depression hit, I had ended an intense and volatile three-year relationship with a man who suffered from bipolar disorder and, for the last half of our relationship, had severe depression. I used to feel so frustrated and angry towards him when I'd come home from work and he would have done *nothing* with his day except build up a relentless narrative in his head ready for a brain-dump on me when I returned home from working with complex individuals. There was no respite, and I resented being his carer and counsellor when he refused to take an active part in his own healing.

Despite all this, and having *thought* I knew about depression, I honestly had *no idea* what it truly was to be depressed until I was in it myself. Only then could I understand what it was and why he couldn't do anything with his day.

I'd slipped a disc in my back earlier that year and was in severe pain for several months. I was signed off work and became bored and frustrated. I found myself just wanting to be looked after. Most of all, I wanted my mum. Instead, I was at home all day with a partner who was so depressed, it consumed all of my energy. Instead of being cared for, I was doing the caring. I knew that he wasn't committed to his own recovery, and, by that time, I was enabling him to continue on as he was. I also knew that I wouldn't recover properly while staying with him. What kept me there was knowing he would try to kill himself when I left.

After a few months of relentless physical, mental, and emotional pain, I left him. I packed my bags and moved to my parents' place. It was such a relief to be away from his energy and to know that I could begin my own journey of recovery.

When I got the phone call informing me my ex had jumped off the roof, I was in total denial that he had attempted suicide. I told myself he must have been manic and thought he was running away from someone. I kind of became an observer in my own reality at that point, and I think I did this so I would feel minimal pain. I had recently had an epidural to relieve the pain in my lower back. Unfortunately, instead of relief, I felt a hot, fiery pain from my mid-back to my neck and all across my shoulders; but it was not physical pain—it was in my emotional body. It actually felt like I was carrying a cross on fire—my cross to bear.

The time came around to go to the doctors for another medical certificate to remain off work. This was a big step for me as I wanted to be working, and I felt awful guilt for my colleagues having to cover my workload. I vaguely remember the doctor telling me I had depression. I went into complete denial mode. I honestly believed I was just in a lot of pain and really exhausted. I only admitted to myself I was depressed when I realized I couldn't read a book anymore, which I loved to do. I would scan the same sentence over and over again but couldn't take any of the words in.

I only had a couple of months left in London before departing for Australia. My family were amazing and such a rock for me, although I knew how hard it was having me around, and I felt immense guilt and pressure to "get better". Not from them, but from myself, so they wouldn't have to "endure me" anymore. My brother became increasingly worried about me and paid for me to go on holiday. So off I went for a week to Turkey on my own, which terrified me, but I knew it would really help. I soaked up the gorgeous sunshine by the pool every day, made some friends, listened to Louise Hay affirmations constantly, and started to feel a lot better.

The day I was able to read a book again made me so happy.

I came back to London in a better state, and after another amazing holiday to Ibiza with my brother and a couple of friends, I really started to feel like myself again. What I didn't allow myself to consider at the time was that I really hadn't dealt with anything at all. This part of my recovery did help me to leave London on a really good note, where I was able to have some cherished last moments with some amazing friends whom I will always be grateful for, and some in particular whom I don't think I would have made it through those days without. These are the people I consider to be my "soul family", and, despite being on the other side of the world, they are always in my thoughts and have a big piece of my heart.

The move to Australia was a whirlwind. I don't think I ever really considered how difficult it would be to settle in a new country. I'd spent so long in London feeling like my heart was meant to be somewhere else. Although I've known since I landed that it was the right place for me, and never did I consider even when in depression that I wanted to leave, being away from the people who had supported me through those darkest days and still loved and accepted me for who I was, was really challenging. Somehow I knew it would all work out but really didn't know how, and some days I found myself panicking that I didn't have a plan B.

When I found myself back in depression, I was in a job, planting trees for three months to get my second-year working holiday visa. I had been in a very on and off relationship, which had started very soon after arriving in Australia. I'd been shown aspects of myself I really didn't enjoy knowing about and felt constantly guilty for. I learned that I wasn't an effective communicator in intimate relationships, although I saw myself as a good communicator in other areas. I constantly questioned and doubted myself, and I became really confused about who I was and whether I was doing the right thing. Anxiety kicked in a lot and it became hard to go out and be around people—a big change for me as I am very sociable.

Since I was young, I've always been the go-to person for my friends when they had a problem, and I seem to have a natural ability to help people feel better and be able to resolve their issues. I've assumed "helper" roles in my work and in my relationships. Suddenly, I found myself working for a visa in a job that challenged me physically but not mentally. Instead, it gave me the entire day to think about my own problems rather than helping others with theirs. I lacked an "escape route" from myself—there was nobody in my life that I was helping. And I plunged right back into depression.

This made me scared. *Really scared.*

Scared of not really knowing who I was at twenty nine years of age. Scared of the negative, self-taunting thoughts that relentlessly ran through my head. And scared of having to deal with the reality that the depression I had experienced was more than just a "one-off".

I realized I was very naive to think that I had left London and quickly put my experiences behind me; instead, I had put it on the back-burner, only to deal with it later when things didn't quite work out as I thought they would. Chemically, my brain wouldn't have recovered from my first experience of depression. I hadn't sought counselling and instead talked things through with my friends. I didn't use anti-depressants either. What I realized during these times was how much of my own self-worth I got from helping others. I'd spent most of my life up to that point investing my energy in other people by being their confidant, counsellor, rescuer, mentor, helper. So many times I ignored warning signs that were telling me I needed to invest some of that valuable energy in myself. With nobody around for me to help, and finding myself quite alone in a new country, I finally had to set out to help myself.

I went for counselling and took anti-depressants for a few months. This was a difficult decision for me to make as I'm a big fan of holistic remedies. I had to ask my family to make the decision for me as, at that point, I was unable to make them for myself. They sorted out my brain chemistry (which was still screwed up from my first bout of depression) enough to make sense of my story in counselling. I started to finally practice what I preach in terms of proper self care, and these days, instead of flinging myself into other people's problems when I should be dealing with my own, I have *Carly time*: sunset walks on the beach, family time, tickling my step-son so I can hear his beautiful laughter, playing with our puppy, meditating, sitting on the beach doing nothing except breathing, and feeling alive.

My story is a very personal one, but one I hope sends you a message—that the most important soulful relationship you can have is with yourself. I feel I am still very much a WIP (work in progress) when it comes to this one, but I'm getting better at it. This is who I am, warts and all. I don't want to portray an image that I have it all sorted out just because I am a coach who helps others transform their lives. That wouldn't be authentic of me. So as you read this, I'd like you to consider the following; where are you investing too much of yourself into other people or situations? Are you "in love" with yourself? Do you show yourself that love on a daily basis in everything you do?

As long as I am making progress towards that goal every day, that is good enough for me.

About the Author

Carly Evans is the creator of Coach Carly, Phoenix Transformation and author of *The Secrets Behind The Secret – The Missing Keys to Manifesting* ebook. Carly supports people across the globe to realize and achieve their full potential through powerful transformational coaching and healing processes using principles embedded in Universal Laws such as the Law of Attraction and Law of Manifestation. Carly also offers Reiki workshops in Perth, Australia.

http://www.coachcarly.com

A DANCE WITHOUT WORDS

Rodolfo Young

There are two voices dancing deep within me. I'd heard one, then the other, in random dialogs here and there, but it was not until I took a full year of silence did I begin to note the harmony of their conversation. It required that I quiet the world around me and within me and that I listen from a space different than the mind.

One voice is masculine and one is feminine. Their language, words, and expression are all distinct if you stop long enough to really hear them, and yet, that distinction has been an effort for me to make for their communion is so intertwined; I have had to listen closely to find which was which.

It was not my choice to stop speaking and go silent. It was an undeniable calling, for those voices sang out without words, beckoning that I listen. And in their soft footsteps, delicately dancing, I heard something profound—something deeply moving; thus, I followed them down a rabbit hole of self-reflection, discovery, and silent inward connection.

Many lessons have been gleaned from watching closely the dancing of this wise masculine and soft feminine inside me. I call them dances for they are not communications by words or speech; they are form, surrender, leading, following, and expression of unfathomable faith, and when you listen with your heart instead of the mind, the lessons sink deep, take seed, and grow from the nourishment of your own soul's divine dancing beat.

Listen from that heart space singing the united rhythms of your own masculine and feminine soliloquy, and, from that place, read onward as I share the lessons I have learned along this journey.

The details of my experience may differ from your own, but behind the stories are dances I guarantee are happening inside of you as well. So, read and let your heart translate the words unspoken.

The Ballet

I paused before entering the villa, my heart poised on a precipice. It hurt more to restrain my love than to lose it all at once.

When I sat, and she found her place across from me, her gaze met mine, and I could tell she was searching for the cause of the pain reflecting in my eyes. I could see her searching to know what to soothe, but it was not my pain I wanted her to find . . . it was my love that sought discovery. My pain was not from any loss or void that she could fill. It was the contraction of my heart that caused such suffering, and its remedy lay simply in my heart being received in open arms.

"Meet me at the shores of some forgotten ocean," I can hear the masculine whisper, "and I shall wash your feet and bathe away your sorrows."

"If I shed my tears, they shall mix within your waters," the feminine responds, "and I do not want to disturb your peace."

"These waters and your tears have come from the same place, the same source. Shed your tears, and let your story be the waves that come and go, for beneath those waves my peace and yours remain," offers the masculine.

The ballet is a dance of strength, balance, and grace. It is a timed coordination paced across several layers of expression. And as those layers unfold, the masculine listens, holds, lifts, and supports, while the feminine opens, releases, and sheds what is no longer needed.

There is no rush, no force, or any prescribed solution. It is a moment-by-moment response of dynamic expressive emotion held in balance by vulnerability. For only the transparent core can lead this dance, and the masculine and feminine must follow that lead in unison.

Vulnerability is more than showing your pain or sensitivity. It is the standing in all the glory of your inner strength and love unmasked, ready to be seen, heard, and held—and fully aware that you already are.

Does your masculine side know to listen, and does your feminine side know how to ask?

For the feminine, it is not an asking by means of petition but, rather, by means of invitation. Express what needs and wants you have as a feminine and the masculine will hear you. If you express only those things not wanted, such as in complaint, the masculine does not know where to support. The masculine wants to be in service of the feminine, his devotion compels him, and he is constantly seeking clues to her deepest desires and needs.

He must wait, stay patient in his solid stance, and give the feminine time to find the words and safety to express what she actually wants.

In devotion, the masculine does not seek to change, control, or possess. For his worship is not of a trophy or conquest, but, rather, his worship is a recognizing, beholding, and appreciating of the feminine before him that gives him his greatest purpose—service.

The feminine must be bold and trusting. She must know his greatest desire is to love her.

How can your masculine hear the questions your feminine dares not ask, and how does your feminine invite him to listen to more than just her words?

The Tango

My eyes were closed, my heart and breath beating to the sweet serenade of the performers as they poured forth their love of the Goddess Saraswati. The ashram was full of people dressed in white, holding prayer candles, silently filling the night.

Eyes still closed, I felt her enter. My heart threatened to escape its prison between my lungs, now breathless. A smile lifted from my lips into my eyes and slowly opening them, I found her there, elegant and radiant, sitting on the steps surrounded by our friends. Her eyes like opals fixated on the performers singing and dancing on stage.

I rose from my seat in the crowd, gently and quietly making my way to her. Gliding through the people, I reached the steps and resisting words of greeting, simply placed a hand on her shoulder as I kneeled in behind her, wrapped my arms around her torso, and let my hands find gentle placement upon her heart.

She covered my hands with her own, our embrace deepening with my chest against her back, our hearts sending secret messages to one another.

I closed my eyes again and imagined the landscape of her smile. I exhaled slowly, feeling the profound love ignited by the distance of a breath and the sweet vulnerability of her surrender in my arms.

"Shall I lay your head upon my chest such that your bed be the cushion of my heart speaking its passions in your ear?" asks the masculine.

"Only if you strip your garments of protections and lay naked so that you may hear the whisper of my sweet sentences upon the vulnerability of your bare skin," the feminine replies.

"I shall embrace you in such gentle yet unrestricted passion that our dance would become one movement of carnal creation," responds the masculine.

The tango is a dance of passion, intimacy, synchronized movement, and absolute surrender to the moment. This dance of two chests breathing as one is both carnal and spiritual, a phoenix of fire reborn in every connected step.

It's knowing when and how to lead as masculine and to surrender as feminine. Her surrender is not a defeat in power; it is rather her gift of trust that he will lead her well.

The Solo

I'd returned home from the concert in the cold night air. My mind busy contemplating whether I should turn around and go to the after party to find her. . . . Was I missing something, was I messing up some Divine providence by not listening? A voice deep within me whispered, "Be patient, trust, go home, and wait."

I checked my messages and emails when I arrived home; a small part of me was still seeking an external signal of what to do. No new messages. I prepared for bed, crawled into my soft sheets, and offered a prayer to Spirit to give her a safe home for the night and that she be embraced in good company and warmth.

That's when I heard the knock at the door. My mind scrambled to consciousness trying to figure out if the knock had been in a dream or reality . . . or maybe both. I stood, shimmied into a pair of Thai pants, and went to the door.

There she was standing in the dark, lit only by a faded moon high in the sky. I invited her in, and as she began rambling about why she was there, I was only semi-aware of her words.

I was more focused on gently removing her motorbike helmet, finding her eyes and smiling softly into them. Her reasons for being there were unimportant to me. I was simply grateful that she was.

She slipped her shoes off, changed into one of my shirts, and, exhausted, surrendered to the soft support of my mattress. Turning the lights off, I joined her, slipping quietly under the sheets. She wrapped her legs over mine, cradled her head in my right arm, and curled into a little ball against me. I closed my eyes, thanked Spirit, and gently brought my breath to match hers as we drifted into peaceful slumber.

"Do you trust that I do not need you to fulfill me, but that I cherish the fulfillment holding you gives me?" the masculine asks of the feminine.

"In moments of safety, when I feel the tension of your Being pulling, not away from me, but rather pulling to hold me in the balance of my own core strength, I can see the truth of your cherished fulfillment," she says, "but when you try to prove your worth to me by showing your strength or worldly knowledge, I lose faith for you are too busy proving yourself instead of listening to my needs. I will always test you, but it is not your worth that I am testing. It is your stability. Can you hear me, lift me, and still remain solid where you stand?"

"I am but the piano keys here to strike the strings that sing your song," he responds, "and there will be times that I lose the harmony and I ask that you trust I have not stopped listening. I ask that you not fill in the missing notes where I have fallen absent, for if I do not hear the gap, I will not know where to jump back in."

"If you want me to trust you, then lead me by your example, not by your stories and supplication. Show me, move me, know me—and I will invite you into my home," she says.

The solo dance is not necessarily about being alone for the masculine and feminine are a pair forever bonded. This dance is about being given space to express while also being witnessed and acknowledged. It is about filling and emptying space dynamically within the relation.

This dance is an act of faith, knowing the masculine is still there holding space for the feminine, while only engaging when she invites him into that space.

When the feminine does not invite or create space for the masculine to compliment her Being, then he is left without purpose, and the masculine without purpose will seek another purpose or simply become frustrated.

Does your masculine hold space for your feminine? Does she let him?

A soulful relationship is found by first knowing the character of your internal relation, the masculine and feminine, and that they do not "need" each other as dependents, but rather can unite in balanced support of each other.

Those two voices, divinely perfect in their recognition of each other's beauty, have no choice but to overflow into the worship of one another, dancing in freedom and connection.

"Let us dance, I will lead, I will follow, we shall make beautiful music with our movement."

About the Author

Rodolfo Young is an international author, speaker, and heart expansion coach who has dedicated the last fifteen-plus years to personal growth, self-practice, and living from his heart. His love of connecting with people and communities has led him around the world, finally settling in Bali, Indonesia, where he completed a year-long silent practice to cultivate connection and expression from the heart.

Rodolfo has led hundreds of people in self-discovery and heart-opening, and through his company, Integrated Potential, he continues his mission to inspire 100,000 people to find their own unique purpose and passion.

http://www.totalauthenticity.com/books

A JOURNEY WITHIN

Sangita Patel

For almost eighteen years, the emotional and physical pain of the car accident that killed my little brother and left me unable to walk had ruled me, inside and out. The pain in my left foot was so excruciating that I could not stand for more than three minutes at a time, and every several months I had yet another arthroscopic surgery to vacuum out the bone chips that had collected in my left ankle, where I had no cartilage.

Why me? Why?

Angry with God, I cried my eyes out. After all the years of surgeries and painkillers, I was not getting any better. My health was only getting worse, and I was putting on weight at an alarming rate. I felt numb from all of the suffering—I could not even feel emotionally attached to my children. I was up to my throat in grief and anxiety. Please . . . no more medications. No more surgeries or needles in my body. I felt like a volcano, ready to blow up. It had gotten so bad that I did not want to live anymore. I did the only thing left to do: I turned to the Universe and prayed for a miracle.

In 1989 when my mother-in-law passed away, my husband, our two -year-old son, and I went to India to put her ashes in the holy river as is traditional for Hindus. My husband went back to the US early to go back to work, but my son and I stayed a little longer so we could bring my younger brother, Niraj, who was finishing his exams, back to the US with us for a visit.

Niraj and I, along with one of my father's employees, were on our way to pick up Niraj's passport at about 7:30 in the morning, when a huge truck—an eighteen-wheeler—swerved head-on into our lane from the opposite side of the highway. Our small car was suddenly under the truck, its roof sliced off, exposing us to further damage. My brother had been driving. My father's employee was in the passenger seat. They both flew out of the car, while I remained stuck—my legs crushed and broken under the seat and my broken bones sticking out of my skin.

Covered in blood and broken glass, I was rushed to the nearest hospital, where doctors treated me for head injuries and prepared to chop off my legs. When my father was finally able to see me, he had me shifted to a bigger hospital in the city, where I remained for the next eight months while surgeons tried to put my legs back together. They reconstructed my left foot and ankle and put a rod in my left leg from foot to knee and twenty screws in my right leg.

I could not see my son during this time because the doctors thought it would be traumatic for him to see me scarred and bandaged from waist to toe, hooked up to machines with my shattered legs suspended in the air. I missed him terribly.

My family, making funeral arrangements for my brother, waited months to tell me about my brother's passing, fearing the trauma would be too much for my injured brain that I might go into shock and coma. When my father took my hand in the hospital room and said gently, "Sangita, I have something to tell you," I knew something was very, very wrong. As he spoke, telling me how—and when—Niraj had died, I felt totally disoriented, like I was listening to someone else's story. What do I feel? How do I feel, when all there is to feel is pain? I had no one to talk to. This loss, on top of the physical pain and the loss of my brother—and my former life—was too much.

I shut down.

After that, I was again shifted to another hospital, where I started to learn to walk again, haltingly, with a walker and crutches. I felt like a baby, having to learn everything all over again. Once I got the hang of my wheelchair, my family brought me back to the US. For the next seventeen years, I underwent surgeries every several months— taking screws out, putting new ones in, taking the rod out, putting the new one in.

By 2005, when I finally reached my breaking point and began to pray for a miracle, my emotional and physical health were so bad that I could not stand living in my own body anymore. I wanted to die rather than have another surgery. But I had also recently begun reading self-help books by Dr. Wayne Dyer and others, and I had an inkling that there might be another way. So rather than let the volcano threatening to erupt inside me sweep me away, I turned to the Universe and prayed: "Help me heal."

All of a sudden, as if my prayers had been heard, I started getting mail about non-Western healing practices and strategies. At a retreat, I met Qigong Master Lin. His vision is that we are all natural-born healers and that anyone can heal one's own body.

That caught my attention.

Qigong is an ancient Chinese healing modality. "Qi" means "energy," and "gong" means working with energy. There are two energies, yin and yang: female and male. When there is imbalance between these two energies, illness, organ dysfunction, stress, even cancer, diabetes and high blood pressure occur. Qigong exercises give positive information and affirmation to one's body again so one can start finding balance. Since I could not stand, I could not practice yoga—I had tried, but the experience was too physically painful. However, I was able to practice Qigong sitting down or even lying on my bed.

As I started practicing Qigong, I was also doing a spiritual course with Master Jeddah Mali, who was teaching about self-awareness, expansion, and living in the moment. Combining these modalities, my life changed completely.

I started to heal inside and out. I had always heard a faint inner voice—it felt like a heaviness in my chest, like someone trying to talk. I began a conversation with that voice. *What's happening? How am I feeling?* At the same time, I was having dreams in which I saw myself as a little girl, six or seven years old, crying in a dark corner.

Exploring my inner self, I found my inner child: that lonely six-year-old whose parents had sent her away from home to school in a city hours away. . . .

All these years I had missed the love from my mom and dad, and from Niraj, so much. At eighteen, I moved away from India to the US to be with my new husband, in a marriage that my grandparents had arranged for me. Niraj was eight years younger than me, only ten when I left, and we had just begun to really know each other. We never got to bond the way I had wanted to.

The darkness that surrounded the little Sangita in my dreams was the absence of the love I had always sensed, and what I had lost in Niraj when the accident took him and my old life with him. I grieved for what that young girl—I—had lost. I reached out to her. I said, *I love you*. And then I cried for about three months just from the relief of letting go and practicing EFT (Emotional Freedom Technique). It was then that I finally processed Niraj's passing.

He is gone. And there is no going back.

Liberation.

Even in my dreams, everything changed. My internal vibration started to rise, and I started to feel more confident, even excited about my life. Okay, I'm here for a purpose on this planet. I'm not just here to cook and clean and suffer.

Physically, I improved significantly as well. The inflammation in my legs decreased, and I could stand up for long periods of time—when I could stand for more than half an hour, it was a huge accomplishment! Clarity finally came within: I have to share this gift with the world—this limitless possibility for healing.

All those years I thought my future held nothing but pain, but now this gift is made clear to me. My present health, both physical and emotional, is incredible. My perspective is completely different: I look at tough experiences as ways to grow, and, more often than not, I live in joy. I give workshops in Qigong and meditation in my local area, and I can stand up for three whole hours. I see a personal trainer, go for massage once a week, eat healthy, organic food, and take supplements instead of drugs—I took my last Advil in 2005, the year I had my last surgery. I still have a couple of screws and wires in my left foot, and that leg is a little shorter and narrower than my right (I lost a couple of bones).

But for seventeen years, I did not know what it felt like to put my bare foot down on the ground. Now I can walk and feel the ground, feel the grass, feel Mother Earth.

We do not have to suffer emotionally or physically. Our bodies are a miracle. We can heal, once the focus turns inward. Knowing your body's systems and your inner self, you can start making the shifts in your body that are necessary for healing. That is how I started. Your healing depends on how open and willing, how committed and responsible, you are.

Everything that has happened in your life did not take place in one moment—likewise, healing is a process. It is like a seed: it takes nurturing, loving care, and sunshine to grow. How open are you to receiving the healing energy of the Universe? The Universe is always ready to help us.

Know the truth of who you are: you are God's child.
You are loved, and you are safe. If you know who you really
are inside, the possibilities for your healing are limitless.

When I felt so overwhelmed and alone with all of my pain, journaling helped me immensely. The act of recollecting and putting it all down on paper helped me understand and finally see my true self.

Try meditation. Try journaling. Try Qigong. Connect with and embrace your inner self to awaken your natural healing power. Ten minutes in the morning and in the evening of these kinds of exercises, every day, will help start the shift within your body to gradually bring you into alignment with universal energy. You will be amazed. Miracles can and do occur. Imagine and commit to healing for you, and you'll be on your way to a miracle.

Every day when I wake up, my prayer is "Thank you, God, for making me your humble and loving instrument of healing. Please send me all your healing energy through my heart to others so I can help them heal." I know that when God comes to ask me, "Did you share my gift?" I can answer with a full-hearted "Yes!"

About the Author

Sangita is a global holistic practitioner. Through her powerful journey of overcoming a life-threatening car accident, which left her suffering with chronic

pain for twenty-four years, she has now come to share these simple and powerful methods of Qigong, EFT(Emotional Freedom Technique), the Holistic Breakthrough, IET(Integrated Energy Therapy), Chakra Healing, and Seraphim Blueprint.

http://www.embraceyourinnerself.com

A NEW POSSIBILITY FOR RELATIONSHIPS

Andrea Osowsky

How different would your relationship look if you had no con-clusion or judgment of what a relationship was? What if staying out of conclusion was the key to completely enjoying all of your relationships?

I remember being a little girl, watching movies and cartoons about these beautiful princesses who were saved and cherished by princes from faraway lands. I remember thinking that was how a relation-ship should be and that I should receive the same feeling from being in a relationship. These princesses didn't have jobs, always seemed to find "Mr. Right" on the first try, got married quickly, and always lived happily ever after. The expectation of the prince on the white stallion was quickly created.

Next, our family dynamics began leaving an impression on me. My dad was fortunate enough to be a part of a family of girls. My two younger sisters and I quickly picked up on our dad's beliefs about young men as he was a high school teacher and once a young man himself. We were taught to protect our hearts and hold out for the prince. Our fantasy was validated and gently settled deeper into our minds.

As we continued to grow into the women we dreamed of becoming, the idea of the perfect man, perfect life, and perfect relationship all continued to linger. We had the ability to map out the type of man we were expecting to show up: his appearance, his career, his per-sonality, and, of course, his immeasurable capacity to love us. We had formed our judgments and expectations of what love was, how it was supposed to feel, how we would know it was love, and what would happen next.

Our fantasy of relationships soon began to break down with every young man we met and with the passing of our dad. And as these fantasies dwindled, our self-judgment became more intense. What was wrong with us? What did the future hold? Were we really as great and perfect as Dad had told us? Asking these questions put me on a spiritual journey in search of healing and understanding of Dad's sudden passing. The more I healed and released, the more I realized how much of my life I had put into my dad's hands. I trusted his judgments and strived to live up to his expectations.

The experience allowed me to grow and taught me how to rely on myself instead of on other people. The gratitude I have for Dad goes beyond anything I can explain. Here are the five keys I have discovered in creating a new possibility for relationships.

5 Keys to Creating a New Possibility for Relationships

1. Trust Your Knowing

My spiritual journey empowered me to follow my own knowing and to listen to my intuition. I learned that the truth would always make me feel lighter and that a lie would always make me feel heavier. I became aware of what was light for me and what was true for me, although it often did not look or feel the way I thought it would. In fact, one of the greatest gifts I received was the awareness that nothing ever shows up the way you think it will. I discovered that all the judgments I had about what I expected to show up actually limited me from receiving something even greater. I got honest with myself and asked myself what I was looking for and what I was expecting. I learned that my willingness to release what I was expecting allowed a far greater possibility in.

2. Stay out of Judgment

I've learned that we see the world through the eyes of judgment: what we look for, we see. This is why your mind can be a dangerous thing. Your mind can only confine and define your limitations. It enables you to see what is truly possible in your relationship because your mind works to make sense of everything. What you have decided is real will continue to show up for you. It isn't until you are able to come out of judgment that other possibilities can show up. Judgment can be both positive and negative, and it has the ability to eliminate your receiving. Whenever you go into judgment of yourself or of your partner, you limit the awareness and kindness possible for either of you.

3. Honor Yourself Without Compromise

Along with learning to honor myself, I also learned about one of the greatest limitations we create in relationships: compromise. How many times have you been told or taught that compromise was the key to a successful relationship? I believe quite the opposite. The more you compromise yourself, the more you divorce yourself. The more you divorce yourself, the more unhappiness and resentment you create. Your willingness to stay true to you is invaluable in a relationship. Now . . . am I saying you should be a selfish "stick in the mud"? No, I am simply acknowledging that giving up yourself in favor of someone else will not create the result you wish to have. If a situation arises between you and your partner that you would typically compromise on, be vulnerable with them and let them know that there is another possibility required for your happiness. In relationships, vulnerability is power. You may be surprised how you are able to have a greater possibility when both you and your partner live without compromising yourselves.

4. Enjoy Your Relationship in Tiny Increments

Sometimes, it can be difficult to be in a relationship without wondering where the relationship is headed and what the future has in store for you two. This, however, can be a huge limitation on your relationship as it adds unnecessary stress and pressure. When you are able to enjoy your relationship in tiny increments—literally, moment to moment—it becomes a lot more fun to be together. Think of your relationships right now—is it more fun to spend time with people who are present, or with those who are always worried about the future? You have got to be willing to be the person you would like to be with. Being present and having the ability to release the past is vital in all of your relationships.

5. Stay in the Question

Asking a question has the ability to open the doorways to possibilities that you have previously been unable to consider. We too quickly jump into judgment and conclusion about what the relationship is, what it means, where it is headed, what other people think, and what is possible. When you ask a question, you receive an energetic awareness that opens up possibilities. These questions are not to make logical or conscious sense; they are simply to create an expansion of possibilities. Have you ever heard of "Ask and you shall receive"? Here are some of my favorite questions to ask with relationships:

> *What would I do or be if I was truly choosing for me here?*
> *What else is possible with us that I haven't even considered?*
> *What would be truly honoring of me here?*
> *What would be fun for me?*
> *Where am I in this relationship?*
> *What would it take for me to give up divorcing myself?*

When you acknowledge that there is no right or wrong relationship, you allow yourself to have total choice. The ability to choose what is best for you in each moment and to follow your own knowing. When you buy into other people's idea of what the right relationship is for you, you actually get further away from your own greatness. You divorce the infinite part of you that knows all that you know. Comparing your relationship to other couples simply creates judgment and resentment. Instead, learn to embrace all that you are and all that you know, by choosing to have gratitude for the gift that you are.

About the Author

Andrea Osowsky is a personal coach and motivational speaker. Her "no-bullshit" approach to coaching allows her clients to dream *big* with wicked confidence and choose joy regardless of their stories. Andrea facilitates high-energy workshops, offers empowering private sessions, and provides the skills required for lasting change.

What would you create if you knew you could choose anything?

http://www.andreaosowsky.ca

THE PATH OF THE HEART

Belinda Pate-Macdonald

Come with me on a journey. . . .

Imagine you're in a cocoon: safe, nurtured, attuned to everything around. You're free, floating in a sea of Love. You're connected. You feel whole.

A spiral of silver curls through you and you know you are being called to The Earth. It's your time. You've been called to bring your special kind of Love to this World. The only kind you can bring. It is unique, carefully crafted by *you* and The Creator together.

It's made up of myriads of experiences—past, present, and future—blended together by the wisdom of your Soul to make a brilliant diamond of Light, which will be your temple for this Life.

The Silver Spiral pulls you gently now and asks you to come into form.

The spark within ignites and you birth into the incredible beauty of Mother Earth. You can feel her diamond light connecting with you and becoming one. As you open your eyes, you are filled with wonderment and amazement as you see the fine gossamer streams of light connection, in a myriad of colors, which links all life together.

There is a radiant glow around everyone and everything, and you immediately open your heart and connect.

Welcome to The Earth, beautiful Soul. We've been waiting for you.

And so starts your path of the heart. A journey which you have chosen to take: to find your perfect place to connect, share, love, and learn.

Remember the wonder of being a child? How you used to reach out in complete trust and touch things? You were connecting, experiencing, learning, and adding your special blend of wisdom to the world from the time you were born.

All this was in complete immersion with the Universal Truth that you have the whole cosmos at your disposal. You can create, manifest, dream, think, dance, and live with magic in your heart.

I can remember this so well when I was a child. The stars spoke and told me that we are all connected. Even though they were so far away, I knew they were part of my family somehow . . . that we could communicate, that there were particles of a magical dust streaming in and around us all, holding us together.

Essence upon soul, from the stars to the Earth, Brother Sun to Sister Moon, and all the planets in between, we are all connected. We are all in perfect, soulful relationship with each other.

So this is where our journey began, and we promised ourselves we would remember our oneness. But between now and then—in the stream of living, learning, and trying to evolve—we forgot some of our amazing gifts.

I know your pain, I know your sorrow, and I know all the things you've tried to keep hidden when you squeezed your radiant energy into the little box that closed around you. I've been there too, trying to find my way into the light, knowing it was there, but forgetting I had wings—thinking I was alone and unsupported.

In an attempt to fit in with the world, I took a side-step and forgot to follow the voice of my Heart. But I knew this wasn't true; it was just a story I made up to learn. And if it was a story, I could change it.

As a separate personality, I wanted to fit in, but from my heart I wanted to soar, to love completely, to be loved, and to be seen from inside out. *To just be me.* So I decided to change the balance of power in my world and give my mind a different job description.

My heart's knowing became my guiding light, and my mind became the wealth of knowledge that could help me take the steps my heart was suggesting. It takes courage, understanding, and absolute trust to let this be in balance—neither dominating the other but being in perfect relationship. And so within myself, I allowed Love to return by making the space for my luminous soul to expand to the stars and back again.

It took many different love relationships for me to understand what I was really looking for. I often chose what seemed to be the "wrong" relationships. They weren't wrong; they were really just pieces of my puzzle that needed to be experienced, loved, and released. Each of these encounters had their absolute gifts and helped me to peel back the layers that had closed around my own loving. Without relationship, we have nothing to reflect back our Love or lack of it. What's in front of us will show us how we're balancing within ourselves.

So I stopped fearing the "wrong" relationship. I knew that the person who stood in front of me was there to unlock more of *me*. I asked my heart if this is where I need to be now to find the key to unlock my heart completely. The key was within me, not something given to me by someone else. The other person simply reflected to me where I could find it. I followed my heart's knowing and absolutely trusted it, even when my mind couldn't understand where it was all going. This is the path of the heart.

Once I found that key within, I could unlock all my past karmic lessons, wound up like an electric ball of fire and buried in my heart. I had carried these lessons into this lifetime to transform and balance. It felt so freeing to bring them into the light instead of having them locked away and being the undercurrent that played out in all my relationships.

Now, this didn't magically stop them from trying to influence my relationships, but it did stop them from having control over me. It changed the feeling of being powerless to being empowered to change. As I surrendered to my heart's wisdom, that divine balance filled all my senses and came to rest in my being.

Eventually, I let go and opened myself completely to create an opportunity to manifest a true soulful relationship: one that was not only a marriage of our dreams as individuals, but also a divine union of spiritual purpose. I knew this was what I wanted and set that as my heart's intention.

Our relationships are the real workshop of life—not just love relationships, but all relationships: friendships, work relationships, communities, global relationships. We need to take that spark of love, our inner wisdom, as a vibrant, alive elixir from our hearts and let it meld with our mind's stories to bring them into understanding, compassion, and purpose.

In this way we can bring our divine essence back into all our relationships. What's so amazing about this is that it fills our own heart when we connect in this way. We release any sense of being separate, guarded, and alone, and we replace it with the remembrance that we are all being drawn together by that sparkling gossamer light that we saw as babies, which is the Fabric of Love. We feel like we belong. We are supported and our place in the world is safe.

When you follow the path of the heart, there are no rules. It is so different to how we see things in a linear world. The heart sees things as connected circles and spheres, all relating perfectly to each other and responding to a Universal rhythm. This is why you will need to let your mind take a rest, so that your wholeness can feel and intuit the rhythm of these circles of life.

Act upon the first feeling you get from your heart. Take that first step and absolutely trust that you will be sending ripples out into these intricately connected circles and that the perfect, balanced response will come to find you. But you must trust, regardless of what your mind is telling you. Learn to listen to that inner voice, knowing, or vision. This is the only requirement of this way of living: always honor your inner wisdom, which is the Love within, and return to your heart if you drift away.

I promise you that if you follow this, you will begin to see how things flow differently to you. As you have the courage to move forward and be open and willing to receive, you will set off a resonance in these sacred geometric circle patterns that creates a clear and strong pathway of flow into your life. Empty yourself of debilitating thoughts and habits, knowing and trusting that you will have more space to receive and fill yourself with Love and Truth.

Bless all your relationships, past, present and future, and imagine them all spinning in perfect balance in the sacred circle of life. You will smile and feel the love in your heart as you understand their place in the whole, and your spirit will dance in celebration that you have come home.

Oh, and did I find that soulful relationship my heart had shown me?

Let me tell you a true story.

I believe in dreams. . . . Not just the magic of following your dreams but the amazing messages contained within dreams while we sleep. They have always been my guide, and I receive a lot of messages in them.

My mother met my father in a dream. She was seventeen and entering university. The day before she was to enroll, she dreamt of my father. He wore all white and carried a pith helmet with red lining, whilst the norm was green lining (she lived in Sri Lanka and this was the fashion).

Well, lo and behold! The next day, there was a mix up at the office and she had to wait with the male contingent of the intake to enroll. There are no mistakes... She saw my father, holding his red-lined pith helmet, duly dressed in white. In her heart, she knew this was the man in her dream and she knew she needed to follow her heart's message.

So you won't be surprised to know that a dream finally whispered to me and showed me clearly who was to be my husband! I was away from my home in Australia, working in Alaska at the time. My friends and I decided to have some fun with crystal cards, so we all drew a card. Mine was Rose Quartz which was all about true love partners.

Considering I had put out this intention, I felt encouraged and excited so I asked Spirit for a dream to show me mine.

That night, I had a clear and vivid dream of my future husband, and my mother (now gone to the Light) was standing with him in her old house. To my surprise, he was someone I already knew! We had been distant friends for a long time.

When I awoke, I could feel my heart's guidance and the message was "Connect!" So I immediately went into panic and wondered how all this could happen. . . . I was in Alaska and about to begin a four-month tour through the States. He was in Australia.

But I remembered I had asked for this. I had made a space in my world for this to enter. My dreams are my messengers and my heart had sent me the sign. I really needed to follow my heart's message. So I took a deep breath and wrote him an email.

The subject line: "I had a dream. . . ."

About the Author

Belinda is a consciousness illuminator who helps you breathe Love and renewal into your life. She is renowned for her gift of seeing your essence and helping you to connect with your true purpose.

Through her work as a heart-centered speaker, spiritual counselor, healer, and writer, Belinda creates deeply healing, sacred spaces that inspire and transform. Over the years, she has helped thousands to discover their own unique and amazing gifts.

http://www.hummingbirdhealing.com.au

WANTS AND NEEDS

Bryan Cobley

People come to me for my healing, Reiki, spiritual counselling, or workshops and courses. I help people connect with their spirituality. They tell me their stories, their hopes, and their fears. Sometimes, I feel that I actually help people. Just a tiny, little bit. I see people grow and change. I see them face their demons. Some people cry and have emotional releases. Stuff they've carried for years. It suddenly comes up and *wham!* It hits them in the face. They have an epiphany. They realize something. Something that they've been carrying all their life. Like a burden. It drops away and, *Gee!*, do they feel better.

Let's face it: at some level, we are all unhappy about something. Even if it's the fact that we are getting older or the kids are growing up and going to leave us alone. Then what will we do? We all worry about something. Even if it's just what others think about us, whether people like us or not, whether we are really good at our jobs, or whether our partner really still loves us. There's always something that's not quite right. Isn't there? Something that, deep down, we know needs fixing.

As we begin to grow, to mature, and to take responsibility, there are times when life can get tough. Especially tough when we begin and take up our spiritual journey. You think you've had it tough? Let me tell you, I've had it tough too. Tougher than most. In fact, I shouldn't even be writing this. Were it not for my father wondering where his car keys were that day, about forty odd years ago, I wouldn't even be here. I'd stolen them along with the keys to the lock up garage. I was in the lock up, sitting in the car with the windows down, engine running; I was hopeless and desperate to leave the world, breathing my last breath and crying in despair. I couldn't live anymore. So tired, so deep in darkness, I wanted to end it all. End the misery.

Three days later, I woke up in hospital from my coma, induced by carbon monoxide poisoning. My father had found me unconscious. My first thought? "Oh no, I've failed." And a deep sense of dread that I had to live. Nine months earlier, I had been in a mental hospital diagnosed with Paranoid Schizophrenia. The doctors had told my parents I would be ill and on medication for the rest of my life. I was going around telling people that I was Jesus Christ. That I came to heal the world. Yeah. Heal the world but couldn't heal myself. Crazy. In the mental hospital they had injected me with enough drugs to knock out a horse. Later on, it was Electro Convulsive Therapy (ECT). That's what they did in the old days. That and padded cells when you fought against the nurses because you thought they were demons coming to take you to Hell. Terror, fear, dread, hopelessness, and—ultimately—tons of self-pity were my constant companions.

The journey back to "sanity" was long, painful, arduous, and difficult. But I made it, and here I am. I'm still "crazy" but in a saner, born-out-of-my-own-suffering kind of way, with a deep compassion for all who suffer. Could that be the way it works? Could it be that what we need to experience is not the same as what we want to experience? I certainly didn't *want* my experience, but maybe, just maybe . . . I *needed* it.

If you think about it, when you make a list of what you want, you are also making a list of what you don't want.

"I *want* to be happy" also means "I *don't want* to be unhappy".

"I *want* to be successful" also means "I *don't want* to be unsuccessful".

"I *want* to be loved" also means "I *don't want* to be unloved".

"I *want* to find my soul mate" also means "I *don't want* to not find soul mate".

Everything you want contains, at the same time, everything you don't want.

Now *that* is crazy!

But let's go deeper. . . .

If everything we want also contains everything we don't want, then we don't actually know what we want.

Think about it. If we are on a spiritual journey, learning about manifesting and creating our reality, life, and experiences, then depending on what we focus on, we create it. Most of the time, we focus on what we don't want, and so we get that. As we gain skill in creating abundance through our focus and intent, we start to get what we do want. Then, when we get it, we want to protect it and keep it. When we do this, we are unknowingly focusing on what we don't want (to lose what we have) and so, sooner or later, we get that.

Is there any wonder that the Buddha saw life as a wheel?

What goes around comes around. We are trapped in this endless cycle of creating what we want and trying to keep it when we have it. It's madness. Insanity! We never focus on what we need. Why? Because we don't understand that every experience, irrespective of whether or not we want it, is always exactly what we need.

Even our experiencing resistance to manifesting what we don't want is exactly what we need because it teaches us to grow. When we truly understand this, we begin to move out of a form and duality-based reality and into a deeper spiritual reality. We are saying, "Thy will be done" rather than "My will be done." In this way we surrender to and accept what is and we pass our need to "control" onto a higher aspect of ourselves.

So here we are on this wheel. Going around and around. Wanting and not wanting, seeking and never finding. This is the world of form: the world of duality. Some call it illusion. I call it a dream—a dream that there is a self that is actually doing something. It's called "free will". You have free will to perpetuate the dream. To perpetuate again and again creating what you want and what you don't want. How do we stop the wheel though? How do we awaken from the dream? Well, if you've gotten this far, then being able to awaken from the dream may not be what you *want*. It's now become what you *need*. You are now tired of this endless dream. Living and dying, being happy and unhappy, loving and being unloved, being rich and poor, gaining and losing. All of these things take place in a thing called "time". You want to go home. It's "time" to go home.

Everywhere around us are "New Age" ideas. Ascension, Enlightenment, Channelling and Guides, Crystals and Pyramids, Angels and Hierarchies, Secrets to creating abundance, Magic and Potions on how to find your Soul Mate, Mediums and Psychics, Tarot and New Technologies—everything we need to create the most blissful and happy life imaginable. Well—what do you want? Is it what you need?

The real secret is to stop it and drop it.

Every experience we have contributes to the unfolding of a beautiful mystery that, as yet, we cannot know. Whatever our experience is, it is needed. It may or may not be what we wanted, but it is needed. No matter how good or bad, beautiful or ugly, small or large, insignificant or magnificent our experiences are, *all* are needed and are of equal value within this unfolding. All relationships are Soulful Relationships because all souls are related to the Divine. "Know that ye are all Gods, ye are all Children of the Most High."

The Universe cannot exist without you. You are needed. You are unique. You are loved beyond imagination. In fact, you are love beyond imagination. All that is asked of us is to be completely this uniqueness which we are. To be it completely—without guilt, fear, shame or neediness for the approval or permission of others to be this uniqueness which we are as an expression of the Divine. To be it in joy, bliss, and wellbeing—grateful for the gift of life as is the child without sense of time or space or judgment of what is. Each of us is the most beautiful creature born out of the Creator's need to express its joy, peace, bliss, and wellbeing. "And God saw that it was good." This is the light which you are. Present in all things. The *dream* is that this is not so. Our *need* is to know that this *is* so. "And the Truth shall set you free."

There are many books out there prophesying in "New Age" terms about the shifts in consciousness now taking place within humanity. 2012 and all that. Talk about what is happening and how mass consciousness is changing! You know about it; you've read about it and you got the t-shirt. Remember that all of these things take place in a "time-based reality". Anything within a time-based reality simply perpetuates the dream of a separated self which has something to do and some place to go. Something to fix. Something to improve. Actually, that's the dream. A dream of a future event of a mass "awakening" of humanity is a dream of a separated humanity. This is not true. We have never been a separated humanity.

For some of us, this mass awakening has already happened. It's not a "future" event.

The idea that we have to "awaken" from the dream *is* the dream. There is only one soul expressed in myriads of ways. The eternal is always present in each and every one of us.

The idea of things taking place in "time" such as "The awakening has begun" and "We have waited a long time" are illusions of the Earth plane where we dream the idea of time and space and create causes and effects. It's because we perpetuate this idea that "things and events take place in time", that we remain unconscious to the reality of our eternity. And so, in the meantime, we continue to dream on asleep to our higher nature.

The belief that there is something to fix or something to "awaken to" or something to "awaken from" simply gives the ego—the separated self—something to "do". It can then perpetuate the idea of itself and remain trapped in an illusion of time, seeking and never finding, because seeking and finding, wanting and not wanting are only the illusions of a self—a self which isn't true. When this illusion of a "self" is shattered, all that remains is the Divine consciousness, and everything already is this Divine consciousness. And, phew, it's okay!

Everything's okay. It was all just a dream.

There's really nothing we have to do. God or "Oneness" never left us. *Love* never left us. *Bliss* never left us. Everything is done. All is complete. No one ever suffered. It was all just a dream. Now we are home and wonder of wonders we never left!

If we can trust in this, if we can surrender to this, then the Divine within us will shatter the illusion of a separated self within us. This is called Grace and the timing is always perfect.

Are you ready to awaken from the dream of separation?

Then stop trying. See every experience as needed. Let it be. "Let go and let God" (or Love or the Universe or whatever you want to call "It"). Become the child again. Allow and trust in the Divine already within you to release that part of you which betrays and denies your deepest desire. Your deepest need . . .

To return to Oneness—a true and *real* Soulful Relationship.

About the Author

Bryan has worked as an electrical engineer and is the co-founder of a successful internet company. He is also a musician, who has played in orchestras as well as teaching the Flute and clarinet privately and in schools. Bryan is a Reiki master, a meditation and awakening-your-light-body teacher, and a channel for guides who assist him with his soul work—working with others wanting to re-discover their inner light, peace, and happiness. He lives quietly and peacefully with his wife, Maureen, in Leeds, UK.

http://www.firstlight.me.uk

MY DREAM MAN AND OUR DREAM HOME

Carol Johnston

2008 was a big year for big decisions and even bigger goals. This was the year I separated from my husband of sixteen years, started to find myself again, and decided what I was going to do with my life to give my two boys the best life possible. It was 2009 that things actually started to come together. I am a big believer in "What you believe, you can achieve," as long as you are prepared to wait for things to happen exactly when they are meant to. The key to getting what you want is repetition. At the beginning of 2009, I wrote down my goals, with no clear way of knowing how they would be achieved.

My list looked like this:

1. To give my boys security: our own home by April 2011.

2. To be happy with someone who loves me for who I am, a partner who I can share my dreams and successes with, and, most importantly, respects me and gets on well with my two boys.

Number 2 did not have a date on it because I felt that I needed time with my boys as a family and if I were to meet someone it would happen when it was meant to.

3. Be brave; believe I can achieve anything and have faith that all will arrive at the exact moment it needs to.

For the first time in a long time I felt happy and contented—everything seemed to just flow. I had a job I enjoyed with flexibility, my bills always got paid on time, and my boys always had food on the table. The only thing that was always at the forefront of my mind was the fact that I was renting and paying for someone else's lifestyle. Every Friday when the paper arrived, it was the real estate pages that would be read first without fail.

I had recently re-read *The Secret* (the most amazing book on The Law of Attraction). I decided to follow a few little exercises; not only did they make me feel good, they gave me hope too. I purchased a Gratitude Journal and started writing down all the wonderful things in my life I was grateful for.

First of all: my family, my two amazing boys, and the fact that we had a roof over our heads—we had somewhere to come home to. I didn't focus on the house being old and the curtains being green and not my taste. For now, this was our home. I had enough money each week to pay the rent and for that I really was grateful. In my gratitude journal, there was also a gratitude intention page; here you give thanks to all the wonderful things that haven't happened yet. This is where you get creative: writing everything you desire in present tense as though it has already happened, just like this:

> *I am so grateful to have my new partner in my life. He is a wonderful man whom my kids adore. We are all so happy. I am so excited to be living in our dream home. We have plenty of room: four bedrooms, a study, two bathrooms, two lounge rooms. We live in a great street with a lovely outlook. My boys are so excited because now we are not renting. We finally have the dog they have always wanted.*

I made sure I wrote in my Gratitude Journal every week, and I also started collecting pictures of houses with features that I loved. The feelings that went with doing this were amazing. The best way I can describe it as is "warm fuzzies". While declaring my desires to the Universe of what I wanted in a house, I was also giving gratitude to my future partner with words like:

> *I am so grateful to have a wonderful man in my life, a man who is strong emotionally, knows what he wants, and uncon- ditionally loves my kids. Thank you for this man who has old fashioned values and isn't afraid to speak his mind. Thank you for this man who treats me the way I want to be treated with love and respect.*

I also did a few other things that came from *The Secret*. I cleared out one side of my wardrobe and decided to switch sides of my bed. This helps to make room for a partner. My wardrobe was clear on one side and I was no longer sleeping all over the bed; there was room for someone else to sleep.

I was diligent in all of these tasks, I knew that everything would happen in the perfect time, and in what order I had no idea. It was March 2009 when I was on a social media site keeping in touch with a friend whom I first noticed: Keith. This was where friends communicate and other people can see your profile pictures and add you as a friend. I can't exactly remember who added whom; however, the one thing I do remember was thinking "He has really kind eyes."

Well, that was it. I eventually decided I didn't really like this social media site, and I started deleting people as preparation to leaving it. However, every time I got to Keith (even though we had never spoken I couldn't delete him), so I stayed a little longer.

Then one day, out of the blue, there was a message: "Hello."

To my surprise, it was from Keith. I returned the hello, and we began chatting to each other via our computers. I found that we had plenty in common, even our marriages ending in the same year. This continued for a few months, and then one day I got really brave and decided to ask him if I could call as chatting on the computer was so impersonal. Luckily he said yes. I think that was about July when we first spoke. It was so good to hear his voice and it honestly felt like we had known each other a lifetime.

Life happily continued. Keith and I were in regular contact. He lived about five hours away, in Canberra; I was on The Central Coast. I continued with my dream house in my Gratitude Journal; however, it wasn't at the forefront of my mind as much as Keith was.

In September, Keith went to England to visit his family. He had immigrated to Australia in 1989 with his young family. He was gone for eight weeks, and, even though we had not yet met, they were very long eight weeks. However, I did get an email every single day which I did look forward to. During the course of his holiday, we both decided that it was about time we met. So when he got back, we did and we finally met in November 2009.

The rest is history.

We had a long distance relationship, which worked. However, it was challenging at the same time. We both did plenty of travelling back and forth. Keith was also retrenched from his job during this time, and I just took it as another sign from the Universe to take a leap of faith—so I suggested he apply for a job here, and if it was meant to be, it would be. He applied for one job and got it. In April 2011, Keith moved in with me and my boys (they both approved and got on very well with him). We didn't just have Keith, we also got his gorgeous dog, Mikey. My landlord approved that we keep Mikey, and my boys were so happy as they now had their dog too.

Going back to my goals I reflected that the one goal I didn't put a date on actually happened before the one I did have a date for. However, the funny thing was that I did have something significant happen in April 2011, so this got me thinking about where I would be in April 2012.

When you ask the Universe for something, be prepared for surprises; sometimes, you just don't know how your wishes are going to be granted or in what order.

I am going to fast forward now to January 2012. Keith and I started discussing the possibility of buying a house together. You see, I still continued my Friday ritual of reading the real estate pages cover to cover. The only difference was that Keith was doing this with me. In February, we saw a finance broker and found out exactly how much money we could borrow to buy our own home. This was a very exciting time. We looked at a few houses but just couldn't pinpoint that perfect house. One Friday, while doing my usual reading of the real estate pages, I actually found a house that seemed perfect, looked fantastic in the photos, and was within our price range.

So, off we went. Unfortunately, the ad was a little misleading and there was absolutely no room for negotiation by the owner, plus the yard was way too small for our gorgeous dog, Mikey. I was a little disappointed, but as we were leaving the property, I noticed the house next door was for sale too. When I looked at it, I got butterflies in my stomach. I couldn't wait to get home and look it up on the internet real estate pages. To my delight, this house had everything on my wish list. The pictures were just gorgeous. My mind was already working overtime deciding where our furniture would go, until I looked at the price: it was $20K over our budget. My heart sank as I really felt this was the house Keith and I would buy together.

I visited that site on the internet daily just to look and ponder. I was just drawn to this house to the point where I would say I am home. This is our home. The house was only a mile away from where we lived, so I just made a point of driving past it. I stopped and looked at it (just the outside). I could see us all living there so happily.

Two weeks later, on a visit to my favourite real estate internet page . . . I couldn't believe it. My heart was racing: the price of the house had been reduced by $20K. *Oh, my goodness! This could be a reality!* We put in an offer and it was accepted.

This is our dream home. We absolutely love it here. I need to tell you the very best part though: this house had *every* single thing that was on my original 2008 wish list and we moved into it on April 2, 2012. You see, the Universe did answer my wish just a year later.

Tips for Manifesting

If you wish to manifest in a similar way as I did, then here are my personal tips for manifesting:

1. Be specific, very specific and detailed. The Universe loves detail.

2. Believe, believe, believe that your wish will be granted.

3. Be persistent and consistent.

4. Spend time every day focusing and taking action on your desires.

5. Focus on the feeling that your desires give you (remember the warm fuzzies).

6. Visualize your desire as if you already have it.

7. Be grateful in the present (what are you grateful for now?).

8. Be grateful for your intentions (grateful for the things that are on their way).

9. Remember to write these as though it has happened.

10. Fall in love with all these processes.

11. Be prepared for your wishes to be delivered in unexpected ways.

Happy manifesting!

About the Author

Carol Johnston is an empowerment, self esteem, and Law of Attraction coach. She is on a mission to help and empower women everywhere, to "rise, shine, and sparkle." Women who have let go of their dreams, women whose lives have become a little ordinary. Women who feel they are drowning in the day to day of mediocre. Women who want their lives to go from ordinary to extraordinary through finding life balance and connecting with their children. Carol also works with tween and teen girls to help them find the confidence to love themselves just as they are.

http://www.caroljohnston.com.au

TRIUMPH OVER ADVERSITY AND THE MIND-BODY CONNECTION

David and Linda Almeida

Linda Almeida

A few years ago, I was admitted to a local hospital with fluid in my heart and lungs. The doctors diagnosed me with a debilitating disease called lupus. I had already been diagnosed with Crohn's Disease, and I was devastated to learn that I had been stricken with another auto-immune disease. It did, however, cause me to take a hard look at my life. My painful situation taught me a very important lesson: our bodies make our life journeys possible. We can't habitually abuse our bodies and expect them to properly function for us.

Crohn's disease and lupus are both painful autoimmune disorders. Crohn's disease is a type of inflammatory bowel disease that affects the gastrointestinal tract and produces a variety of severe symptoms in that area. Lupus, on the other hand, is a disease in which the immune system becomes hyperactive and attacks healthy body tissues. The excruciating symptoms of lupus can affect a number of different body systems, including the joints, kidneys, heart, skin, cells, and lungs. I have systemic lupus—which can affect any part of the body—where the immune system attacks the body's healthy cells and tissues; this can cause a dangerous inflammation to occur in a person's vital organs, which ultimately leads to tissue damage and death.

I have spent a long time reflecting on my life and can honestly say that I was mistreating my body. I wasn't eating properly, exercising enough, or tending to my self-care. I gave my body the minimum attention needed to keep it running. I was not putting myself first, or should I say "not at all". I was working at a very stressful job that didn't inspire me. It certainly wasn't related to my professional career goals. It was an unfulfilling job, which I tolerated to pay the bills.

My life was in disarray, and I felt the vitality of my body slipping away.

My recovery was slow and required a lot of mental and physical effort. I was not always motivated to push forward. My life and schedule had become crammed with doctor appointments and medical treatments. The treatments were meant to deal not only with the symptoms caused by the diseases, but also with the some-times severe side effects of the medications. I was truly unhappy with the turn my life was taking and was confused about what I wanted for myself. The only thing that I *did* know was that I did not want to be sick anymore.

After much soul searching, I realized that I wanted to create a life filled with joy and happiness. I realized I did not have to wait until I felt better to have the life of my dreams. It was simply a matter of choice. I immersed myself in inspirational books. I enrolled in online classes and workshops that stirred my passion. It was a period of self-discovery for me. I knew that I had lost myself and that this inner exploration would help me find it again. And so I decided to allow myself more fun and freedom.

I found it helpful to keep a gratitude journal. I wrote down all of the things that I loved and was grateful for in my life. It took me a while, but I realized that when I focused on the wonderful aspects of my life, I began attracting experiences that filled me with joy and gratitude. My life was turning around. I started to feel better about my circum-stances. My change in attitude was making a tremendous difference.

I realized that I was communicating a new message to my body. I was telling my body that I cared about it and that I wanted to be healthy. In doing this, I was establishing a soulful relationship with my body. My body responded positively to my change in attitude. Somehow, it understood that I no longer wanted to suffer from its dysfunction.

Once I started recovering at an emotional level, my internal energy increased. My body began to function normally. I was walking every day. My physical stamina improved and my symptoms were man-ageable. I began to clear out all of the physical clutter in my house.

In the process, I discovered some malicious emotions that I had buried deep in my subconscious. I wondered if there was a connection between my repressed emotions and my Crohn's Disease. I kept this thought in the back of my mind and continued to work on myself.

Meditation and breathing exercises gradually became a part of my daily routine. As I quieted my mind, my body relaxed. It felt wonderful. I was feeling better, and the exercises helped me to manage many of my dreadful symptoms. My life was coming together. I started to see all of the possibilities forming in my future. My life had become better than I could have imagined. It was a stark contrast from my long period of illness.

I had acquired a positive outlook on life, and an amazing soulful relationship with my body.

Throughout this healing process, I was inspired by many well-known personal growth authors and lecturers. In time, I earned my M.Ed in counseling psychology. I also graduated from Coach University and became a certified Law of Attraction coach through Quantum Success Coaching Academy. When I look into the future, I see the possibilities, and I reach for the ones that I love and that inspire me. My mission is to teach others that they retain the personal power to improve their lives, no matter how dire their circumstances may be. Life can be either pleasurable or unbearable. The key is in your thoughts and in the choices you make.

David's Supportive Comments

Linda's testimony concerning her experience with mind-body healing is certainly inspirational. Her story exemplifies the vital relationship that we as spiritual beings have with our physical bodies. We can see from Linda's personal testimony that our bodies require respect and love. The body is more than just a mass of organic matter used to house our spirit while we traverse the physical world. It is teeming with life from the small cells to the larger organs. Our bodies are comprised of multitudes of much smaller organisms, giving them the complete form we see in our mirrors. Every anatomical unit identified by medical science has its own consciousness; I would include in this statement the individual cells, the organs they form, and the systems themselves.

The Dynamic Mind Body Connection

The world seems alive. A person with an acute awareness can sense the vibrations of love and life radiating from all around. All living creatures and even seemingly inanimate objects possess consciousness. This is not empirically evident nor is it endorsed by the scientific community; however, anyone who has been awakened to the true nature of reality can feel it all around them. This experience leads to the understanding that the Divine is embodied in all creation. In fact, creation is a living expression of the Divine. The Divine is a being of total love. All physical manifestations of the Divine are imbued with its high vibration.

Our bodies are equally one with the Divine. The units that comprise our bodies are healthiest when this desirable vibration is circulating throughout their systems. We call this favorable condition *homeostasis*. Any discord or unresolved mental conflict leads to disease. The members of the body can sense the stress being internalized by the human consciousness. They will react to this state accordingly. The reaction the body gives to psychological stress is usually unpleasant. The body can even breakdown. The signals we send to the body through our brain and central nervous system tell the body to defend itself from attack. Prolonged exposure to overstress or repeated trauma takes its toll on the body. One does not need to refer to clinical research studies to appreciate this statement.

There is a misunderstanding about stress. If you mention the word "stress" in a casual conversation, it typically translates to "a sense of discomfort" to the other person. A certain amount of stress is, however, good for the spirit and, therefore, good for the body. People are meant to exert themselves in order to experience personal satisfaction and success. Stress is also always equated with pain. However, this condition is usually only true with overstress. Stress manifests itself in the challenges we must overcome to experience that wonderful growth that helps us improve ourselves. Everyone, in any condition, can challenge themselves in some way. Even if you are physically disabled, it's still possible to find some activity that gives you pleasure and a sense of purpose. This practice is extremely beneficial to your body.

How does this achievement-building process help your body? Well, anything that is beneficial to our personal growth has a positive effect on our bodies. If you are passionate about something, chances are you will welcome a challenge that comes your way. By following your passion, you will overcome these challenges and, in the process, improve on your character. Your body will also reap the positive effects that your mind is registering.

By reflecting on Linda's compelling story, we can understand the truth of this statement.

If you are suffering from a terrible disease, there is a way of mentally talking to the different conscious members of your body to correct the issue. As always, living creatures—and even inanimate objects—respond best to affirmative language. Your body is no exception to this rule. Positive self-talk heals your body. Your body systems, organs, and cells sense your affection and love, just as much as your negative thinking sends it into disarray. By talking positively to your organs, you are showing love for your body. Your body needs this reassurance to maintain homeostasis. People can actually reverse some of the worst medical illnesses by being good to their bodies, just as Linda was able to. Your body reacts to your thoughts and emotions. It will either do its job correctly or have a malfunction based on the signals it receives from your mind.

It's as simple as that.

This positive self-talk can be combined with creative visualization to enhance the experience you have with your body. Creative visualization is incredibly powerful and has many uses. Visualization is used by hypnotists to create positive changes in people. Linda used this very technique to manage her Crohn's Disease and lupus. Other well-known auto-immune diseases are fibromyalgia, ulcerative colitis, celiac disease, multiple sclerosis, chronic fatigue syndrome, and narcolepsy. Having a loving relationship with your body is an effective treatment to all of these illnesses and so many more. Treating your body with respect and dignity may not only help you to better manage your illness, but it may also cure you. Please understand that I am not a physician and that this is *not* medical advice.

Many people look at their bodies in the mirror with disgust. They wish they could have the body of a fashion model. This sends a dangerous message to your body. If you were to tell your mate that he or she is fat and ugly, how do you think that statement would affect him or her? Your body is your best friend. Like your mate, your body will react negatively to such criticism. Linda learned this lesson well.

She discovered that her bodily consciousnesses needed her nurturing as much as a child requires his or her mother's encouragement to develop normally.

The bottom line is this: positive self-talk will result in a desirable soulful relationship with your body, and a healthy outlook. Finding fault with certain features of your body will lead to disease. My recommendation to everyone is that we should accept our bodies and give them thanks for being good friends with us. From there on in, your countless body consciousnesses will eagerly work to keep your body in a healthy state.

About the Authors

Linda Almeida is the owner of Find Your Light Coaching. Linda is a Certified Law of Attraction Life Coach. She received an MEd in counseling psychology from Cambridge College in 2000. In 2008, Linda graduated from Coach University. She received her certification from the Quantum Success Coaching Academy in 2011. Linda is committed to helping others realize their unlimited potential.

David Almeida is a Spiritualist and researcher of Rosicrucian philosophy and esoteric knowledge. He is also a Board Certified Hypnotist, certified past-life regression therapist, and Reiki healer. David is the author of The First Truth: A Book of Metaphysical Theories and Illusion of the Body: Introducing the Body Alive Principle.

http://www.findyourdivinelight.com

THE LOVE OF MY LIFE

Angela Ambrosia

Early one year, I asked the universe for "The Love of My Life".

I was teaching a workshop about how the relationships we attract in life are often *not* the relationships we dream about but rather experiences of love where we can learn about our unique understanding of love. Asking for "the love of my life" doesn't guarantee that you will manifest a love relationship. The love of your life may be to learn how to love your *true* self, to learn how you desire to share love, or to learn both. Your true self knows what love is. And your true love, the "love of your life", is often different from your personality's interpretation of love.

At the time of the workshop, I had been breaking up with my exboyfriend after we had decided to separate in January 2010. It was the longest break up I had experienced! And in those two very long years I had explored every reason why we had to break up.

The questions why he didn't want to be with me and what stopped him from loving me were continuous. *What's so wrong with me that he can still sleep with me but can't have a relationship with me? What does he mean: "I don't know if I want to be with you"? Don't you just know when you love someone? Isn't that what love is? Why can't he just love me?*

On the outside, everyone around me was wondering why I couldn't move on. They saw we had irreconcilable differences and that parts of our relationship were not that great. So, logically, it was better for me. What they didn't understand is the deeper process going on inside of me, trying to understand why I felt so connected to him and why we could not make the relationship work.

A few months later, I started a daily meditation to connect to my soul. I had always felt very soulful and thought I knew this part of myself. The difference of meditating with the soul is that after a while you hear a voice that has been waiting for you to listen, so it can then *respond*.

When my soul started speaking to me in my meditations, I was surprised to hear this wise voice inside of me, so different to the nattering of my mind and string of endless questions. The voice of my soul was calm, clear, and precise. I started to get answers to all my questions.

The soul's answer was simple: *You are not able to be together because you are still awakening the part of you calling to be fully seen. With him, you will be able to do so but only once he has established himself as fully recognized in his own being. At this time, you remind him of how he is incomplete, not the fullness that both of you know is the life gift you both strive for.*

I felt a comfort in knowing that this wisdom traveled with me just as much as—and more than—the constant mind chatter that wanted to know if I would or could be with the love of my life.

The process of letting go of my ex-boyfriend became a dialog between his soul and mine. I felt the connection between us so strong because we both wanted the same thing: the liberation of the other person without sacrificing our beliefs in love.

We kept thinking that we had to sacrifice something to get our love.

And the lesson for both of us was that *any* sacrifice does not allow love to flourish.

What was confusing was the feeling that there was a deep bond and affinity between us. That bond and connection was our need to resolve the need to sacrifice in order to love.

Sometimes, you can mistake a soul lover as a life-long partner or as the love of your life because the bond is so strong between you. The bond is, however, so strong because there is a lesson that both need to learn to fulfill their soul growth. Both of you share in teaching each other the lesson; that's why you are together.

After a year or so I still had an attachment to him that I couldn't shake. I was far away in another country and would still feel him. I wanted to move on—I had got the lesson—but my thoughts would still go to him. There were still *"What if it could work?"* scenarios in my mind, yet I knew that the relationship was done.

So I began a conversation with his soul that asked him to let me go. I figured that I had talked to my own soul so much through my meditations that I may as well connect to his in meditation as well.

The results were powerful.

In meditation, I visualized the two of us coming together where souls meet and converse. If you wish to do the same, you can just ask to be shown where this place that souls can connect is. Some of you will already have that gift of going into meditative or contemplative states and connecting with those close to you at the soul level. Everyone has their own version of heaven; the soul is designed to teach you lessons, truths, and meanings that are unique to you, and your soul uses images of spirit and heaven that will be specific to you. Sometimes, we have universal images that we all connect to in meditation. The fastest path to your soul is to ask for the connection. Your soul is always ready to feel you when you are ready to open up to its energy.

When I met him in meditation, I asked why I had to be still connected to him at this soul level.

I was holding so tightly to a life-long dream of disappearing into the one I love and being embraced in a love that would support me no matter what. This dream was my desire to give, be, and receive love so fully so that I could feel completely at one.

By "breaking up" I was crashing my dreams of finding "the one" and destroying my dependency on finding love from somewhere outside of myself. It was not losing my boyfriend that hurt as much as losing the sense that I could connect to this greater love that I know exists everywhere—if we just open to it.

Even though I felt unable to be myself in the relationship, I was still attached to being with someone who felt like such an old friend and who I could—at moments—sense this connection to the greater love within and around us.

I continued the conversation with my soul so that I could totally understand why he wanted to hold on and why I could not let go. And I asked him to help me let him go. After the meditation, I felt sad but complete. My sense that I needed him in my life was totally gone. I went to the ocean and released my tears. There was a sense that finally this connection was ready to be closed.

The meditations with my soul allowed me to open myself to the abounding love that is in everything I do, and it set me free from feeling only one point of love through my last relationship. My soul was ready to expand beyond any limitations of love that I had conceived of since a child. My concept of love was expanding into a greater sense of the universe and my place in it. I am just ready at any moment to feel the power of love moving through me . . . if I just let it.

I had more conversations with his soul over the next year to fully forgive any hurts and sense of loss that had passed between us. When you have a "lesson" of sacrifice to learn between souls, the tendency is to blame the other partner instead of taking responsibility for allowing the sacrifice of yourself. I realized that we often set relationships up so we can work out our stories of where we feel cheated or let down.

I also was very good at playing rescuer in my relationships so when my partners walked away I could complain how they didn't appreciate me.

The truth is no one needs to be rescued. Rescuing someone does not equal love. It's your attempt to cover up what you really need to work on. My soul had made a good story of rescuing others because I so wanted someone to make me their own and prove that great love was there for me. I thought that "helping" was a way to express love.

What I really needed to pay attention to was to stop sacrificing what I truly wanted in love just to have a relationship with someone, as if that could prove that the great love I was looking for did exist.

When I wrote my first book *Body of Love*, it was after a year of communicating to my soul and feeling the abundant love of myself flowing through me. The book poured out of me like a universal amorous love fest of all the potential love that I had found in my body, dance, and joy. I started writing six months after I had put that request out to the universe for the love of my life.

Writing the book was like a preparation for what was to come. Once I fully acknowledged the great body of love inside of me, without any attachment to a relationship, then the relationship could naturally enter into my life! And so it did.

It was nine months after I made my invocation for the love of my life that I met my new love. From the moment I saw his face online, I felt my heart smile. From the moment I saw him in person, he felt like a dear old friend. And he also felt the same sense of having met before.

With my new affection, I thought I was finally free of my past. But in the awakening of this new love, all the residual anger, frustration, and confusion came to the fore and flooded through my body! In encountering a new love, any final fears of being left behind without love were coming up to be cleared. I was grateful that I had the wisdom and experience of my soul to tell me exactly what was going on. In a final soul meditation I released my fears of not being able to create the love I desired.

We often fear losing that which we want the most. Never let your fear of losing love convince you that the love you desire is not possible. It is just old energies telling you that love is full of failure. But love is *also* full of success. Instead of seeing failure, how do we create the love we truly desire?

My new love and I are still exploring how to expand our sense of who we are. We still have our challenges. We definitely have a soul mate connection and often drive each other crazy!

Every day is a challenge and an amazing possibility with my new love. Every day, we aim to fully recognize who we are as individuals and celebrate, support, and accept the other person. We are stepping into a new version of love that many couples are experiencing in these changing times. It is one where, as two individuals, we create a relationship that supports us both to be fully who we are without sacrificing anything or anyone: standing in the fullness of love and knowing that love is what we are here to create, treasure, own, and celebrate.

About the Author

Angela Ambrosia is a spiritual coach, healer, and author. She specializes in teaching people and light-workers to reprogram their body to love. Author of *Body of Love*, she has over twenty years experience in dance, performance, and energetic healing. Angela's teaching encourages freedom through understanding the body's messages and desire to unite spirit, sensuality, inspiration, and love. Her students find clarity in their intuitive knowing and authentic connection in their relationships. She has evolved an advanced energetic healing that uses intuitive listening to the body and emotions so they can be accepted and flow and create loving dynamic relationships.

http://www.dancewithangela.com

LOVE IS ALL THERE IS!

Gezim Dancja

I was having coffee in my garden one warm summer morning, and, as I was looking around, I felt like nature had prepared a special show for me. As with a great theater performance, I was overwhelmed with the beautiful display nature had prepared, with a cast of blooming flowers, the waltz of bountiful tree leaves, and the array of colorful birds.

The freshness of the air, the smell of the awakening flowers, and the singing of excited birds caused my mesmerized Soul to leave my body and embrace the moment. After that orgasmic moment, my eyes took a break by watching the young family of kingfisher birds that had hatched in their nest in the far corner of the garden. As I watched them busily feeding, it reminded me just how similar we are!

Like the birds, my wife and I had been busy with our three kids in our nest: our house. With that thought in mind, my Soul came back into my body. Soon, another thought took over my mind: that we are all one; we are an extension of the Source energy. We are literally God expressed in this physical body. Therefore, we can choose to be or do anything we desire. We don't need to belong to any particular group, race, or religion to fulfill our desires—all we have to do is tune in and align with Source energy, with who we really are.

And that's where the question hit me: *So, who am I?*

Am I just my name, my body, my color, my nationality? Am I my language, family, society? Am I my religion and my beliefs? Or am I something else, something more and above all that I know, see, touch, taste, and feel in this physical body?

My life journey knocked on my mind's door and shouted, "Of course you are more than just this body you've been carrying around all these years! Rewind the movie stored in your memories and pay attention to details to get your answer."

As I looked into my life's movie, I remembered that I am the creator of my own life in this physical reality and that there are two parts of me: the physical part, which is what my body represents, and the broader nonphysical part (my soul), which is just an extension of the Source energy itself.

I came to understand that in all ways, consciously, subconsciously, or unconsciously, we are creating.

Our dominant thought creates our reality, and one of the most powerful universal laws, the Law of Attraction, brings all the circumstances together and makes sure that our dominant thought is manifested in our reality. My life journey gives me more than enough evidence about how laws of the Universe conspire to manifest my dominant thoughts in my reality.

Our thoughts are vibrational energy with different frequencies. The Law of Attraction states that you attract what you vibrate to. Think of it as a Genie from a bottle: "Your wish is my command!" Because I was always attracted (vibrated) to the culture of the Far East with all its beauty and mystery, the Universe brought together two Souls from two different corners of the planet: me, from beautiful north Albania, and my wife, from exotic South Korea. Two souls with different looks, language, and culture were joined together in Great Britain, through the glue called Love. The love then started to blossom and bore the fruit: our kids. As I was becoming more aware of the power of the Law of Attraction, I became more conscious of my dominant thoughts and what I was asking for, as thoughts become words and words become things.

At that time, our dominant thought was to have a girl, and before long our first daughter came along. Then we thought that it would be nice if our daughter was to have a little sister to play with. Two years later, our second daughter came along. Then my strong desire was for my daughters to have a little brother; again, two years later, our boy came into this world. At that time we felt we were complete and that our dominant thoughts became our reality. I came to understand that we were a tri-part being, made of body, mind, and spirit or soul. The soul conceives, the mind creates, and the body experiences.

We were excited, as we understood that we can manifest *anything* we desire, as far as we think it—visualize it—and then let it be. We decided that we do not want to live our life at the effect of our experiences; we wanted to be the cause of them.

And *that* is conscious living.

We agreed at the conscious level that the purpose of our relationship was to create an opportunity, not an obligation—opportunity for growth, for full Self-expression, for lifting our lives to the highest potential, for healing every false thought or small idea we had about ourselves, for looking into the positives in each other and building on those, and for ultimate reunion with Love, through the communion of our two souls.

I wanted our journey to be filled with passion, as passion is the love of turning being into action. It fuels the engine of creation. It changes concepts to experience. Passion is the fire that drives us to express who we really are. You are what you experience. You experience what you express. You express what you have to express. You have what you grant yourself.

Soulful relationships will thrive when love feeds your heart, like the sunshine kiss to the flowers in the cold summer morning. When you wake up in the morning and look at your wife's sleeping eyes that seem like two beautiful red roses, this is bliss. When those red roses slowly open to their majestic beauty, their vibrant colors hypnotize you, their aroma draws you like a magnet—you inhale deeply and the pleasures smell travels through your veins burning with desire, awakening your soul, which shouts, "Ah, I love you!"

That love became the bridge to my successful business life, the fuel to my entrepreneur spirit, the safe and supporting bridge I could cross over, whenever the waters of life would come with a challenge! That love made the two of us become one, embraced in each other— and that energy beamed from us like a golden light. That energy created the third entity—our kids, the crown of our love!

Love is all there is!

About the Author

Gezim is an author, mentor whose aim is to help people from all walks of life to achieve their dreams, and an ambitious entrepreneur with a desired focus and experience in online marketing. Gezim believes that we all deserve, and have the ability, to live our life fully, to experience an abundance of wealth in every aspect of our life. He also believes that it is our God-given right to experience and enjoy the wealth of our beautiful planet.

http://www.gezimdancja.com

SOUL BIRTHING:
A DOORWAY TO INTIMACY

Binnie A. Dansby & Lynne Thorsen

*"All my relationships are an expansion of
the relationship I have with myself."*

Everyone wants satisfying relationships. We tend to look for them outside of ourselves. We think they are elusive. Our perception of Relationship is based on the fundamental, essential, and often unconscious relationship we have with ourselves. To better understand how relationships work and gain insight into our relationship patterns, it can be helpful to explore and heal the source of our perceptions and conclusions about relationships. As a result, we can clear the barriers to who we really are. We can free the one who desired this body, this life, and this journey. This is the process we call "Soul Birthing"!

We began this lifetime in the body of another, our mother. Binnie calls this relationship "the original intimacy". A growing body of evidence in prenatal and perinatal psychology supports the fact that we are educable in the womb. We not only "made up" our bodies, but we also made up our minds. Research in the field of medical neurobiofeedback shows that in the womb and first year of life, the brain is operating at a level of theta and delta brainwaves. From the age of two to six years, the child's brainwaves are mostly theta: the frequency related to imagination and the state of hypnosis. Bruce Lipton, an eminent cellular biologist, refers to this primal phase as "the download phase"!

We form beliefs and make decisions that create the default operating programmes and patterns that become active in our lives. We were awake and aware of what was happening in all the relationships around our Mother. Our mother's actions and interactions with the world, our father, our family, and our friends were "first contact" for us. Her perception and her experience of relationships have an influence on our perception of our experience of relationships throughout our lives.

What we learned from "the original intimacy" is the origin of our thoughts about connection and separation, about intimacy and isolation. How we were received and treated both physically and emotionally at birth and in early childhood continues to expand with each new experience. The influence on our perception of Self and the world we live in is profound. We create subconscious operating programmes based on these early experiences. They are held in the body, at the level of the unconscious mind. For most of us, many of these early programmes are negative and not appropriate to who and what we aspire to be. Until we bring these early negative thoughts and beliefs to conscious awareness, we are victims of the decisions made in the preverbal state.

As we progress to adulthood, we develop our own wishes and desires for who we want to be and what we want to achieve. These wishes and desires are held in our conscious mind, and while we focus our attention on them, they can become our reality. The problem arises because it is estimated that we only spend five to ten percent of our time fully engaged in our conscious mind and ninety to ninety-five percent of our time defaulted to the hidden programmes and patterns of our subconscious that were created by the thoughts, actions, and ideas of others during the preverbal, primal phase. We call these programmes the "hidden saboteurs". As a result, we struggle to reconcile what we want in "relationship"!

> "The conscious mind's prefrontal cortex can process and manage a relatively measly 40 nerve impulses per second. In contrast, the 90 per cent of the brain that constitutes the subconscious mind's platform can process 40 million nerve impulses per second. That make the subconscious mind's processor 1 million times more powerful than the conscious mind's."

The good news is that we have the ability to heal and change these negative programmes. Healing begins the moment a life-diminishing thought changes to a life enhancing one! Each time we heal a negative belief or decision, we are re-sourcing the relationship that we have with ourselves. Giving birth to the Soul who chose to be here in the first place, the Soul who came to love and serve, the Soul who desired the full sensory experience of being in a physical body.

Binnie:

"What is the matter with you?"

A question I remember often hearing as a child when I was discovered crying alone.

My answer was usually, "Oh, nothing."

I was unable to say that "matter" (the physical) was the matter with me. My body hurt. Mother, my incubator, spaceship, guru, doorway to human life was also in pain. Our conflict was classic. Fear and confusion blocked full expression. Desperately sad, I was always aware of a deep longing for something or someone and did not know why. Time and "the adults" taught me how to manage the feelings. I learned to suppress them. I learned to name homesickness and heartbreak and disappointment. I learned to project them out onto other people or situations as the cause.

I experienced real growth, release, and relief in psychotherapy and group therapy with a noted psychiatrist. I also participated in new alternative forms of personal development available in the early 1970s in New York City. There was still something missing though. I did not access the true source of my longing until my first session of "re-birthing" in the strange environment of hot water with a snorkel and nose clips. This form of breathwork was in the very early stage of development. It was thought that the activator of birth memories was the hot water. I know now that it was the breath, slow and steady through the snorkel into my wounded heart, that activated the birth memory of guilt and sadness and shame. I felt excruciating physical and emotional pain in all of my body about my mother's pain. My words through the body's wrenching sobs were "I didn't mean to do it. I didn't mean to do it."

That was a life-altering experience for me. I was deeply impressed with the power of the process and the link between body and mind through the breath. I continued to explore birth, birth memories, and the all-important breath as the pathway to the memories held in my body/mind. My relationship with my mother changed dramatically. I was more able to accept and receive her and her way of showing love. Once the barrier of guilt was revealed, I embraced my own innocence and love for my mother that was primal and eternal.

I realized that my intentions are pure and always have been; my loving expression is safe; and—oh so crucial—those whom I love are safe with me.

I had retrieved a part of my Soul. The longing was for my body and my love, not hers or someone else's. I wanted to feel my body wholly without fear, to be wholly with it. I knew that my longing was to fully individuate, for matter to materialize Spirit. I sensed that I had begun to consciously fulfil Soul's Desire: to embody love, to serve, and to enjoy the experience of being physical. This is an ongoing process that informs all of my life.

Being aware that "My love is innocent, my love heals!" has made it possible to do deeper self-exploration. This knowledge has facilitated both emotional and physical healing. I know that awakening to the essence of being innocent and the truth of my loving intention in all things has allowed me to be in compassionate relationship with myself and to support others on this shared path. A fundamental loving relationship sustains the ability to create successful relationships and, also, to face challenges in Relationship, whether they are personal, clinical, or physical.

Love is all that matters in the fullness of time.

Lynne:

Several years ago, I embarked on a journey of self-discovery. At the time, I was living in victim consciousness, as I perceived that "others" were the source of my unhappiness. My journey began by analyzing the traumatic and negative experiences that I had conscious awareness of and by exposing the negative beliefs and decisions that led me to attracting these experiences in my life. I have documented this part of my journey in my previous chapters in the *Adventures in Manifesting* titles *Healing from Within* and *Passion and Purpose*.

I was aware that there were still more layers of negativity to uncover as some of my key relationships, although improved, continued to lapse into periods of dysfunction and highly charged emotion. During a guided "Soul Birthing" meditation, I uncovered a deep and pathological guilt. This guilt stretched back through the aeons of time, infiltrating my consciousness and physiology and ready to be activated by experiences in this lifetime. During my gestation, my parents were still trying to deal with the grief of losing two previous babies (deformed foetus and stillborn). With little opportunity to express and process their grief, their emotions were supressed and internalized. Several times over the years, during meditations or breathing sessions, I have received awareness that I had been that stillborn baby.

My guilt was activated by this. It was then compounded by the fact that my mother was so ill during the pregnancy that she was hospitalized several times. I decided that I was making my mother sick, literally! In my mind, it was my entire fault that she was grieving, horribly ill, and unable to take care of my father or brother. By choosing to take on this guilt, I created a life where I had to either defend myself against being wrong or accept punishments to atone my perceived guilt. I unconsciously judged myself harshly to avoid the judgment of others. However, in order for me to be right and avoid punishment, I had to make others wrong!

During my next Source conscious breathing session, I felt so loved and supported that I resolved to trust and really surrendered myself to the process. I experienced an extreme physiological response where my lower right leg was paralyzed for fifteen minutes or more as the stored negative energy was freed. I then had tingling sensations for more than three days as the energy began to flow again. Conscious awareness of this guilt was simply not enough to completely let it go. I also needed to physiologically release the emotions that I had stored deep in my cellular structure. When I surrendered my guilt both mentally and physically, I was able to respond from love and compassion rather than from fear and guilt. The results were instantaneous. I was no longer "reacting" with my old negative subconscious programmes to the people that I was "in relationship" with. Without the need to defend myself, I began to create loving solutions.

This experience has allowed me to understand how our physical body is ultimately an expression of the energy in and around us, including all thoughts and emotions. I have learned the value of healing at both a psychological and physiological level.

Empowered change, emotional freedom, and manifesting your dreams all begin with this process.

Binnie & Lynne:

Life is a co-creative process. Who we really are is consciousness that co-creates! We are always in relationship with the people, things, and places that we contact, no matter what we have or say we want. In an expanded awareness through meditation, guided visualization, and connected conscious breathing, we are actually connected in consciousness to all that we can conceive. Relationship is a moment-to-moment event, and each of us has a choice about our thoughts and, thus, attitude about any person, place, or thing. Our thoughts and behaviors may be sourced in the past or we can look again to see what is real in the present moment. We have a choice!

As you embark on your own journey, some universal truths to remember are:

- Thought plus energy creates results.

- Like attracts like!

- What you give attention to (positive or negative) always expands!

- Love brings any thinking and behaviors that are unlike love to the surface so that they can be changed and healed.

It is imperative to understand that who you are is not any of your thoughts. Who you are is the *one* who chooses what to think and the *one* who chooses how to use your energy. You can choose to create new life-enhancing thoughts to replace any that are life diminishing.

This is your true power! This is where healing begins!

About the Authors

Binnie A. Dansby is an inspiring teacher, gifted therapist, healer, writer, and philosopher. For over thirty years, Binnie has been developing her SOURCE Process and Breathwork therapy, educational programs, and courses. These form the basis for the online healing system, "Soul Birthing", which she has co-created with Lynne Thorsen, to facilitate the safe and effective release and healing of the life-long wounds of fear, inadequacy, and limitation.

Lynne Thorsen is an intuitive healer, therapist, and freelance writer/blogger on self-empowerment, healing, and natural birth. Her inspirational stories have been published in a number of print and online publications, including two previous *Adventures in Manifesting* titles.

Binnie and Lynne are also the co-authors of *Wake up to the Impact of Birth* and offer online healing programs at their website.

http://www.soul-birthing.com

SIREN SONGS AND SYMPHONIES

Teresa Powers

One question I'm often asked is whether I see the world as a glass "half full" or "half empty". My experience starts with first being happy to have a glass at all . . . even if it came slightly chipped.

My life didn't start with the typical beginnings of eager anticipation from my mom as she welcomed her first child into the world. Instead, it started with frantic hustle and bustle three months earlier than my expected due date. Just over a two-pound birth weight, I desperately gasped for air with lungs that were barely prepared to handle even the smallest of breaths.

I not only came in on my own terms, but I also broke the mold in ways. Upon delivery, my dad had to face the decision to tell the doctors to amputate a few of my fingers from my left hand after they found them entangled in amniotic bands, which left those fingers deformed and nonfunctional. A similar fate my right foot would have suffered if I hadn't expedited the delivery process by coming out early. My fight in this world had begun.

In hope that I would simply make it through the night, my parents quickly whisked me away to another hospital where proper equipment was available. My survival was in question on an hour-to-hour, day-to-day basis. My parents were faced with the sobering statistical chances of survival that were stacked against me, delivered with a tone that showed little faith from the doctors that I would make it at all. If I lived, they were told, there was also the grim picture portraying a challenged life with brain damage caused by the multiple episodes where my lungs gave up and started to dance with death.

Death, brain damage, and chronic respiratory issues didn't seem to be in my cards. However, prejudices, ridicule, shame and emotional challenges would be. The most important relationship in life is, first, with oneself, and my journey wasn't going to be an easy one.

During the early years, a child begins to establish their foundation of self-esteem, personality, and confidence to keep them afloat throughout life. I faced the challenge of being different from others with the visible deformity most noticeable on my left hand; by the time I was in kindergarten, I had started to have skin growths develop on my eyelids that were impossible to hide, which helped me feel even more grotesque. It may not seem like much, but even the slightest abnormality tends to make people uncomfortable. The emotional daggers thrown my way cut deep . . . no matter how small the blade or the wielder.

Shy, I hid my hand in my pocket until my mom, cleverly, started buying pants without pockets, knowing that hiding it would do me no good. My parents were supportive but knew I had to go most of the journey on my own. When I started school, with each new class, I was uncomfortably exposed and vulnerable as pint-sized strangers would respond in shock and ask me what happened to my hand. This only drew even more attention from other classmates to where I felt exposed and at the mercy of others. I was feeling victimized by the unpredictability as to when attention would be called to my hand or eyes. I was also feeling utterly alone not knowing anyone with an amputation or deformity.

I even faced emotional abandonment and a sucker punch to my esteem and sense of worth when my sister was born "normal and perfect: ten fingers and toes" (of which I had neither digits).

In hindsight, I realized by the time I was in third grade I was already a tumultuous cesspool of emotions. The responses of shock, or silent judgment, from children and adults made me feel I was something to be ashamed of, broken in the eyes of others, literally less of a person. I remember questioning why I was different, wishing to be normal or to disappear, all the while clinging to the fantasy that my fingers would one day grow back, only to have that dashed by the reality that they never would. I had multitudes of examples of people and society telling me what I couldn't do, rarely telling me what they thought I *could* do.

I had only one true friend whom I let in, starting when we met in first grade. She was my saving grace. I'm sure other kids tried to be closer to me, but my inner bully was having fun, splashing around in the toxic emotions convincing me to keep them at a distance; it convinced me that other kids only wanted to be my friend because I was a curiosity or because they felt sorry for me like a carnival side show. My friend was my beacon of hope and made me feel "seen".

Tragically, our friendship was cut short when she died in a plane crash when I was only nine. I didn't understand why God would take someone "perfect" and leave me instead, when according to doctors I wasn't supposed to live at all.

To me, it was another example of how I didn't deserve good things. I plummeted as survivor guilt added to my darkness. I'd be lying if I didn't say there were numerous times I entertained the idea of welcoming a way out of life if death came knocking . . . all the while too chicken to bring it about myself.

My self-defeating dialog sang its siren song and became louder as it harmonized with anger, bitterness, and resentment. For so long, I listened to the song within. Suffocated, my soul had finally crashed into the rocks and was thrown into the unforgiving emotional sea gasping for air. Sink or swim.

My true self was stifled like the premature babe that I was so long ago, gasping for each breath. It was then that I realized I hadn't really been living at all. I had lost faith—not just religious faith, but faith in myself too. All along, I gave in to the toxicity of a self-defeating existence every time I looked at life through a victims eyes and asked "Why me?"

I was finally tired of people telling me I couldn't do something because I was a girl, a minority, or because I was small or missing fingers. I was tired of believing other people had all the answers, and that is when I started to look for answers within.

I first started looking through my internal muck trying to figure out who I was and what I was going to keep as my truth. Some of the same questions I had throughout the years like "Why was I born this way?" or "Why me?" evolved and shape-shifted as I asked out of curiosity versus distress. It was easy to pick out my inner critic voice as it was one I was too familiar with. So I started to listen more closely, and that is when I heard the whisper of a voice I abandoned long ago. That is when I started to find myself.

I asked again, "Why?" And like an echo, it responded with "*Why?*" Confused, I re-approached and asked again "W-H-Y?" The answer that bubbled to the surface was simplistically complex. The "Why" *was anything I wanted it to be...* so again it responded, "Why?"

With that one question, my awareness started to expand, and I realized things weren't as black and white as I previously believed. Over time I had a playful sparring match with this newfound internal voice that started to quickly gain importance over my critic. This voice, this knowing inside, challenged me in new ways by constantly pushing me to find meaning where I once thought there was only pain.

It helped me to start finding my true self: the child I had abandoned long ago. More and more, I matured with the knowledge it helped me connect with—much like a child that was screaming for attention that finally gets the comforting ear from their parent. My soul was finally being heard.

My inner world started to change with rays of light and hope shining where there were once only shadows. I started to reconnect with faith. Faith that there was something more to the world around me, as well as faith there was reason and purpose for all the events of my life.

I no longer viewed them as a burden, started to own my life, and no longer hid who I was. The more that I was open and exposed, the less people seemed to notice my deformity. It didn't define me.

The stares and reactions didn't disappear completely. However, I now openly brought it up and chose to, instead, educate people through my example. I had noticed how trivial issues and events would almost make people buckle and collapse, which helped me realize how my new attitude towards life made me feel empowered and find my strength. I had gone from victim to feeling humble and grateful for the unique lessons I would have only been able to learn by my life circumstances.

I no longer danced to a siren song; instead, the song had matured and changed to a beautiful concerto . . . and I was the conductor. Melodies ebbed and flowed through my being that was filled with love, joy, and strength. The more I danced to the new tune, the more beauty and joy entered my life.

I went on to accomplish things like earning a second degree black belt in Tae Kwon Do, started to teach others, and even won a bronze medal at the junior Olympics as a teen. I found and married the love of my life and helped him change his own siren song by using the healing ability of love. I was able to heal wounded relationships by first healing the relationship I had with myself. I now encourage and offer support to others affected by Amniotic Band Syndrome. I am humbled to life coach and spiritually counsel clients to live a more empowered intuitive life by finding their own voice within.

Much like a painter, we all have unlimited potential for creativity, and our future is a blank canvas. The emotional residues from various events in our life are like the colors we work with on our palette, and, as the painter, you have full control of the colors you work with. Listening to what others tell you, and seeking out answers outside of yourselves, can leave palettes riddled with black, white, and gray tones. Throw away any templates and sketches that have been thrown at you and create your own masterpiece of finding more color and beauty by opening up your eyes to seeing the world from loving eyes. Starting from the love you feel within, seek out the most vivid and outrageous colors you can!

We all have struggles and events in life that can be tragic, painful, difficult, and shaming. We're all trying to navigate through the difficulty of being human and we all have siren songs, some more haunting than others. Some have learned how to see the beauty that hides in between the notes and melodies of a song. What matters most is what song we choose to be the soundtrack and theme song of our life. Make the choice to grab the conductor's baton to create new melodies and harmonies to waltz to. Dance to your own symphony. Paint your own masterpiece.

Lastly, embrace and feel gratitude for the imperfections in your life. For I truly believe "Imperfection" *is* "Perfection". "Imperfect" is an illusion, and the truth is that "I'm Perfect" already, and so are you. Our relationship with ourselves is the anchor for the happiness, joy, and love that ripples throughout our lives. So let's toast to our success, our chipped glasses happily in hand, filled with the gratitude for simply having a glass.

About the Author

Teresa "Romana" Powers is a professional psychic intuitive that helps clients all around the world through personal readings and life coaching. She blends her passion and knowledge of psychology with metaphysical knowledge to empower people to reach their highest potential. She founded the Facebook Group "Mission: Intuition" to encourage, support, and connect like-minded people as they explore the spiritual world around them. A strong believer in community involvement, she teaches metaphysical classes and workshops and also volunteers her services to help local charities and nonprofits.

http://www.ourpsychicpowers.com

CHANGE YOUR SHOES; CHANGE YOUR LIFE

Celia M.

Somewhere between being struck by a car and the ambulance ride to the hospital, I seem to have lost my shoes, my life, and who I was.

My story . . . starts somewhere.

On October 28, 2006, my life as I had known it came to an end. As I attempted to open my eyes, the light was blinding. . . . I didn't recognize my surroundings. Was I dreaming? I tried to focus. "She's awake," I heard someone say—then a flurry of voices came from all directions. My head and body felt like they had gone through a meat grinder. Where was I? "You have been in a terrible accident. You are going to be okay," I heard someone say as if they were hearing my thoughts. It was a familiar voice: my sister's. What was she doing here and where was I?

What accident?

Over the next few weeks I would learn that, crossing the street to a friend's home and getting struck by a car, I had suffered serious life threatening internal injuries: I had multiple broken bones and my right elbow was destroyed; I had sustained a brain injury and had received over fifty-four units of blood; and I had been given a trial drug. The list of injuries went on and on, so I had not been expected to live. And Christmas was only two or three weeks away.

In a blink of an eye, I went from a completely independent, physically fit, career-driven, adventurous fashionist to a pajama-wearing, withdrawn home body who was completely dependent on others. As weeks turned to months and months turned to years, the pain and torment at the loss of me pre-accident did not lessen. At times,

137

it seemed even more painful than the physical pain I dealt with every day. Everyone tried to assure me things would get better, but each time I looked in the mirror I saw a stranger in the reflection that looked back at me.

As autumn 2012 approached I pretty much was giving up all hope and could feel myself slipping into a very dark place. I neither loved nor liked the person I saw in the mirror. If that's how I felt about me, how could anyone else love or like me? I retreated to the safety of my home, venturing out mostly for medical and therapy appointments only. Perhaps life would be much better for those around me if I simply no longer existed were the thoughts that occupied my mind.

Ego once again started taking over, creating fear—telling me *I couldn't do it, I was not good enough, what could a person like me with a brain injury have to contribute to the world? I was no longer worthy of good things or good people in my life.* Sitting in the oversized lounger in my bedroom with teacup in hand, I began to feel even smaller and everything about life started to feel out of reach. Yes, I was having a pity tea party of one, and Ego was dishing out some pretty toxic bites into my thoughts.

Trying to shake my thoughts, I began to look around the room. My gaze stopped at my beautiful high heeled shoes neatly lined up on shelves staring at me, pleading to be worn once again. Before the accident, it was a rare occasion to see my feet in something other than high heels. At 5'2", that extra inch or two—and sometimes three—made me feel like I could conquer the world, and I often did. Now, traces of dust lingered upon them. It had been years since my feet had slipped many of them on, let alone tried to actually walk in them. They had been replaced by granny slippers and sensible walking shoes—translation: flats.

> "Give a girl the right shoes and she can
> conquer the World." – Bette Midler

Looking at my shoes, my thoughts drifted to happier times—recalling the moment some were purchased or how each one had been the crowning accessory to one of my outfits. Making my way across each shelf with my eyes, my thoughts were interrupted by a book that had been tucked against the side of one of the shelves. Ah, *The Secret*. I remembered receiving it in the mail, shortly after returning home from the hospital in 2007, as a gift from my sister. At that time, I could barely remember a sentence let alone think about reading a whole book.

Though I had watched the DVD a couple years back and tried to recall its message, reaching for the book I could not have anticipated what would happen next and how it would affect my life. Casually opening the book, my eyes landed on a paragraph on page 71: the first page for the chapter *Powerful Processes*. The three-line paragraph read, "Your current reality or your current life is a result of the thoughts you have been thinking. All of that will totally change as you begin to change your thoughts and your feelings." Standing in front of the shoe shelves I must have re-read that paragraph a dozen times. Thinking about the words I'd just read, I wondered if I could be keeping myself trapped in these circumstances.

Somehow, at that very moment, I knew I had to change my thoughts if I was to escape the darkness that had taken hold of me and had become my reality. I would need to rebuild the loving, caring, nurturing relationship with myself that once had come so easily. Unsure where to start, I decided to make a list of people whom I admired: Oprah, Maria Shriver, and Coco Chanel were among the names I wrote. Then, something moved me to add my name to the list. I started to reflect on how far I had come: from laying in a coma with no expectation from the doctors that I would survive to breathing on my own and living. The passage from *The Secret* ignited a survival fire within me like no therapy or friend could have. Then it hit me that when the Universe had been screaming at me to hear its guidance, I had allowed Ego to dismiss its loving messages as foolish thoughts.

For the first time, I could see and acknowledge that while I made everything look great to the outside world, inside where no one could see I had been emotionally dying at the hands of my own thoughts. I started to see that my flat shoes had enabled me to take small, tiny steps forward, but there was much work to be done.

The task began with consciously becoming aware of all my thoughts. When a negative one snuck in, I began to find ways to replace it with a positive one. On mornings when getting out of bed seemed next to impossible, instead of wishing the darkness to come, I changed my thought to "How blessed am I to be alive for another day?" Instead of thinking I have nothing to offer others, I thought of the listening ear I was able to offer, the time I could spend with them, or the story and lessons learned that I could share. Turns out, I *did* have a lot to offer others.

I now think about how deserving I am of wonderful things and people in my life. When I started liking and loving myself, things and toxic people who were not for my highest good began to detach from me in an almost magical way.

Once my thoughts were in positive alignment, my actions towards myself started to also take a more positive and productive role. Instead of just sitting with my daily cup of tea for thirty minutes, possibly encouraging Ego to plant unconscious, negative fear-driven thoughts, I use this time to visualize the wonderful people in my life and the great life I'm living. (Even if it's not quite here in its entirety, think positive; make your thoughts in the present.)

When I look in the mirror, I no longer focus on the scar that now graces my once tone and smooth abdomen, the scar on my throat that took away the pitch in my voice, or the scars that enabled me to keep my right arm. Instead I see these scars as a gift from above because without going through what I have, I would not have a story to share with others. Through my experiences and survival, I am able to help others build a soul-relationship with the person who is with them their whole life here on Earth—themselves. I know it sounds like a cliché—but everything does happen for a reason. We need to stay positive, keep the faith, and believe that we are never given more than we can handle—even in our darkest hours, all we need is a flicker of light to create a new direction in our life.

"The most important relationship in your life is the relationship you have with yourself. Because no matter what happens, you will always be with yourself."
~ Diane von Furstenberg

Perhaps the biggest lesson I have learned so far on my journey is that in life you will wear many different shoes with varying heel heights. Some will help keep you close to Mother Earth and others will raise you high towards the sky. No matter what shoes you are currently wearing, know that you are taking steps toward discovering and creating the life you are meant to live: a life of purpose—of giving and helping others—and it all starts with the fabulous soul-relationship we create with our self.

Once you have built a strong, loving, and nurturing relationship with yourself and begin to think positively, you will bring to life the fabulous relationships you dream of having with others. You will also be able to ignore the fear-based negative thoughts Ego uses to keep you from being your highest self.

In my high heels, I was living a very fast-paced, corporate lifestyle with little time for me. The Universe had been trying to get me to slow down; when I didn't listen, it literally knocked me out of my heels. The greater this relationship with myself becomes, the more my dreams become my reality. I was even wearing wedges on a regular basis. With positive thinking and building a strong soulful relationship with myself, I have changed my shoes and started creating the life of my dreams. And you can too!

"My life didn't please me, so I created my life." – Coco Chanel

About the Author

Celia M. is a certified life coach, author, blogger, inspirational speaker, and student of life. Since 2010 she has been inspiring readers (from 173 countries, and counting) of High Heeled Life to take time to truly live and enjoy each moment in their day.

She firmly believes living a High Heeled Life is not about excess: it comes from achieving balance and peace within our self (mind, body, and spirit). Once we have peace and balance, we are able to create and live our personalized version of a High Heeled Life.

http://www.highheeledlife.com

THE BURNT CHILD

Helen Herfurth

She is standing there all alone. She is afraid. She is lost and she is very lonely.

This little girl throughout her young life, and into adulthood, has felt alone with little or no support.

Today, as an adult, I can still see her standing there vulnerable, looking around in an empty room, unsure of where to go, what to do, or how to go about it.

She was the only child to a couple who were immigrants to this country of Australia. They worked hard to make a good life and to provide the material things. From a very young age, the little girl was frightened of her father as he was an aggressive and emotionally abusive drunk. It was at this time that his rages always aimed at mother and child.

The little girl's mother was subservient to his drunken tirades and demands and was frightened to put a foot wrong—no comment would be made when his aggressive abuse was occurring, which was more often than not!

There was no nurturing, support, or love in that dysfunctional family home—only fear: of when the next drunken tirade would be. The mother who was a beautiful soul did the best she could: she showered love on the little girl—"But don't tell your father," she would say—behind closed doors!

What the little girl needed was to feel safe and secure and to have love and support unconditionally and openly, but sadly that was never to be, as the fear of her husband was too great for her mother to support her child!

The little one never felt safe or secure and was frightened and sick to the stomach. She dreaded going home from school on a Friday as the father would be drunk and verbally abusive. This kind of behavior would continue all weekend. The poor little one and Mother would live in constant fear. There were times when they hid under the house to get out of his way.

There was another traumatic memory that had a much greater impact on the frightened little one. As the drunken rage continued, he brought an axe into the house as a threat. It was then that Mum and the little girl hid in the bedroom with the door locked to escape his tirades. Even though the axe was never used, the threat of terror was there, which had left the little one very frightened, indeed, again!

What remained throughout the turbulence of her home life and into her future was her happy disposition. Even though the hurt had cut deep into her soul, which she carried with her, she remained optimistic and happy outwardly.

She always hid behind her mask, as not to be seen or heard, and she hid what she wanted to say or how she felt.

The words "Don't speak your truth. Hide behind the mask. Don't stand out. Don't let yourself shine," were imprinted in her. As she heard them time and time again, they had a huge negative impact on her development.

Even though the little child had no positive memories at all of her young life, she was happiest when the father was at work, as he worked nightshift. The mask would drop off then, and life would be "normal" for a few short hours!

That is very sad really.

Friendships away from the house were not encouraged. There was one particular memory that stands out as this event was one of many that worked against the young teenager's development.

When the girl was in her early teens, as the father worked nightshift, he slept most mornings. As this particular time was school holidays, the young teenager had a friend from school come visit; not to disturb the father, because he would be cross if he was disturbed, the girls decided to go for a walk. Well, little did they know that the father was awake, was aware of what the girls were doing, and was very suspicious. He jumped into his car and chased the girls, catching up with them, screaming and swearing at his daughter all these obscenities under the sun. He told her that she was up to no good as she was prostituting herself! "Get in the car! You are going home!" he said. Her young friend was left to make her way to her own home alone. How embarrassing and belittling.

This was a pattern in this young girl's life that would appear often. There was always suspicion from the parents and she would be wrongly accused of all sorts of immoral acts mostly by the father and, on occasion, by the mother, only because she wanted to live a normal life, to do normal things that normal people her age did, like meet up with friends, go to parties and nightclubs (when of age), and be called a prostitute again!

She was a good kid, and being accused of having the morals of an alley cat did not sit well, as it was not true. Actually, the thought was never on her radar. She *just* wanted a normal life!

She remembered stories by her mother of when she (the mother) was a young girl and what a great social life she had!

It was never understood why the girl wasn't given the same freedom the mother had and why there was so much aggression towards her wanting to have a normal, innocent social life with her own friends.

With the unhappiness of her home life, there were a few times when the little girl ran away from home to the neighbor's house for the day without telling anyone where she had gone, as there was no other family she could go to for refuge, away from the drunken madness at home. At the neighbor's house, she would play with her friends until it was time for lunch. Their mother then scooted her children into the kitchen for lunch, told the little girl to stay outside and wait on the back step till they finished, and closed the door on her! There she was again: alone and not wanted.

The mother's actions' significance was realized later in adult life during the writing of this story. The mother in her warped thinking instilled in the little girl that your opinions, hearts desires, and dreams don't matter: just who do you think you are to want those?

In consequence to this, decisions and choices that would be made in the future would be made out of fear, not passion: fear of being judged or criticized, fear of being roused at from parents or other people for making that decision.

Unfortunately, her hearts desires and dreams were never encouraged or considered. She lived her life doing what others expected of her until she was in her forties.

With the father's constant instability and the mother's denial, the little girl developed a real fear of aggressive raised voices and of speaking her truth. But, again, she went and hid from the drunken wrath of her father, hiding the little girl within herself what was truly going on. She conducted herself through her life in this manner. She hid from the truth.

It was not until well into adult life and therapy that she understood that, yes, you do have a right to voice your opinion, to speak your truth, and to be confident in giving it—that your hearts desires and that dreams do matter. Yes, you do blow your own trumpet and not to feel guilty in doing it!

So this sweet little girl hid behind a mask. She hid from the triads and hid her opinions, desires, and dreams. This frightened little girl grew to believe that you are not worthy of value. Her confidence plummeted as time went on.

From the innocence of childhood, the little girl took with her all her insecurities and injustices into her adult life.

She was happiest way away from home. School and friends at school were a salve for her.

The young adult conducted her life as she only knew how: "Don't speak up! Don't have dreams and desires. Live in fear."

Career aspirations and goals? "What is that?" she would say. You don't look at the future. You survive another day in this dysfunction.

Around this time, she developed an eating disorder. At times of stress, this is how she coped. She was alone again with little or no nurturing. She lived her life in fear again.

Even though there weren't any positive role models in her life, as life was not at all easy for the little one, her abundance of love remained. She maintained a positive and happy attitude throughout her turbulent home life.

Empathy for the underdog was very strong and she could not tolerate people acting in a dishonorable, unethical, and dishonest manner.

She felt very deeply when people were hurting, as her intuitive abilities were heightened. She understood it because she had been there.

Unknown to her, deep in her subconscious, there was this passion to assist others who have experienced unjust, bullying behavior like she had. Then it hit her when she was in her forties. She recognized that in changing her career, she could—and would—change the course of her life forever.

Remember, she still wore that mask. The confidence was not there for her to say too much about her change of thinking and direction to take her life.

Even though the little one had a traumatic home life, and she carried the pain with her throughout, she soon realized that if it wasn't for her life experiences, she would not be in a position today to be able to assist and nurture, to be empathic and understand other hurting souls.

As hard as it is for her to say, and for others to understand, she now thanks her parents for the lessons that, otherwise, would not have brought her to where she is today in assisting others.

She now knows why she is here, what her role is on this Earth. She now knows she is here to assist others, to share her knowledge, wisdom and to empower women globally. Sure it has taken awhile, but she is here now.

The memories of The Burnt Child will always be there, but the impact of the hurt has lessened.

This is not what the little girl had set out to do with her life. All those years, she didn't have her vision set to doing anything at all, because she did not know how to dream.

What she has learned is how to rise above adversity, follow her passion, and turn Her Wounds into Wisdom!

About the Author

Helen Herfurth was born to nurture and empower other people to face their challenges in life. After experiencing adversity in her own life, she felt she has the understanding on how others were hurting.

Reaching out to beautiful souls like your own is very exciting for her. It's her passion. She is now able to assist others in sharing her knowledge through her business.

http://www.justkickitnow.com

FEELING THE FEAR AND LOVING ANYWAY

Claire Timmis

I enjoy people! They fascinate me with their individual passions and perspectives and the wisdom they so often illuminate in my soul. I celebrate the individuality of each person I meet, for that is what makes them unique and keeps my life exciting. I view every meeting as an opportunity to learn and to grow from within, whether that person ruffles my feathers or sings to my heart, I bless them and know that I am better for having met them, on some level, at least.

I haven't always been in this mind space of acceptance, I confess. Not at all! It has been quite the journey to get here! But the shift I eventually made into realizing that life is truly a process of co-creation, and therefore everyone in my life is here as part of *my* plan, was the greatest gift I could have given to myself.

This recalibration within my understanding of self had a ripple effect throughout my world, and I can honestly say that all the current relationships I hold near and dear are truly soulful connections.

In fact, soulful connection is a prerequisite for becoming a part of my inner circle, and I have no shame in sharing that (and nor should you), because when relationship energy flows as it should, life, love, and laughter simply happen.

The Bumpy Road to Me

The truth is, my own marriage began with two wilful beings marking territory and staking claims within our home, until a beautiful baby girl arrived and I fell out of the rat race and into making home.

Motherhood didn't come naturally to me, I confess.

During my pregnancy, I had delighted in absorbing every pregnancy magazine on the shelves, and I couldn't wait to meet my baby. Yet, when the time came, these same magazines compounded my confusion as *I didn't feel anything* but sore, exhausted, and constipated (in every way possible).

How could this be?

I, myself, was raised by a beautiful, but very tired, mother, who was diagnosed with multiple sclerosis when I was four years old. Despite this, she fought tirelessly to make ends meet, whilst my alcoholic father drained all resources and, ultimately, all warmth from our home.

Feeling unable to leave the torrid situation, my mother closed down to her heart's desire for freedom: emotionally, mentally, and spiritually, until eventually her body closed down too.

I learned all relationships involve struggle.

The mother to daughter advice handed down to me mainly revolved around negative reinforced ideas from her own experience. "Never become trapped in a relationship," was a regular piece of well-meaning advice. I heeded her word and began all my relationships in defensive stance.

Of course, in truth, this meant that the only relationship I was trapped in was the one with myself.

When it became my turn to be mother, the loneliness of childhood was revealed like an old septic wound, and I just didn't know how to connect with this beautiful baby in my arms. This demanded a deep love way beyond anything I had ever experienced and I simply didn't feel qualified. This baby demanded that my heart must open. And she demanded that it must open *now*.

Yet, I didn't know how to open my heart. What I expected to be a natural instinct of mothering this beautiful child just didn't light up for me, and with my heart closed to the voice of my soul, I felt so alone. I transformed my feelings of loneliness and guilt into bitterness toward my husband. It felt like the death of my dreams and freedom.

I was unable to escape from my self-imposed prison. I had to either deal with the pain or sink further down, as I had, by now, completely shut down every part of myself to my husband and the world around me.

With little spiritual maturity, I didn't understand the potential in my situation to truly, deeply heal.

Being tired and crabby simply compounded my self-pity. As I was so closed down, my only true relationship was with myself, and I didn't like her very much—at all. My life and relationships were functional at best.

Baby number two soon arrived: a joyful little boy. Things actually became more orderly and practical with two children than with one. It was lovely that the children had each other and that love flowed between them.

And I didn't really feel my pain anymore! It was now more of a convenient numbness! I was still closed down, but, at least, I had morphed in a way that others could approve of me. I was wearing clothes, I brushed my teeth, and, of course, the kids were clean and fed.

When an opportunity arose for us to emigrate to the greener pastures of Canada, we took it. However, this, of course, completely cut our family unit off from everyone we knew. Feeling unable to integrate into my new surroundings I spent most of my time indoors. I was happy to be with the children whilst my husband had a successful career, and soon our spirited third child was born.

Then, in a moment, everything changed.

Our youngest son was diagnosed with leukaemia, and a three-and-a-half-year intensive medical protocol followed. We were experiencing the ultimate holding space and were completely paralyzed as time stood excruciatingly still.

It was as though a great Universal clock was hovering over us: tick tock, tick tock. Yet, what I understand now is that each tick reverberated loudly in time with our hearts, bringing us back into tune with each other. There was no choice but to become present and grow *up* and *into* ourselves, both as individuals and as a family team.

It was our most difficult, heart-wrenching experience, yet the passage, ultimately, led us all home. The gift of this holding space and our son's ultimate remission was that we all found each other in new, purified light, and we have been rewarded with a family and life reborn. I'm delighted to say we are now all healthy and reconnected.

I found gratitude. I found forgiveness. I found joy and celebration in life that I had never experienced before. My son is now nine-years-old and has more energy than anyone I know. My heart is open, and I can finally see my family for the amazing blessing that they always were. The rest is history, as they say.

Revelations: Opening the Heart

What I realize now is that I always had a family of soul mate relationships. My husband and I were simply not soulfully connected but focussed mainly on the mundane experiences in life, seen through the filter of our parents' vision. We needed to find our own vision from within.

I see now, too, that my husband had always supported my dreams unconditionally; yet, as I wasn't fully aligned with myself, I was unable to see this and projected my expectations of people into my own main relationship.

In retrospect, it was easier to believe that any blockages in my life flow were coming from my husband rather than look inwards and face the fears I had in stepping out and trusting life's flow. It took near tragedy to fully realize that what was missing all along was within me.

Humble Musings . . .

Soulful relationships are created when two people are mutually supportive of each other, without compromising their own life experience. Within this relationship, one person can look at the other and see the path to their happiness and heart-felt success and be willing to light the way. This is because a soulful relationship is not based on co-dependency in any way; instead, it is one where two people experience each other through the heart and recognize themselves in the reflection.

True heart connections are created when we begin to shift into living our own truth and choose to stand firmly in our happiness. When we are authentic to our path and voice of our heart, there is no need to communicate with anyone, ever, in any way but from the heart.

Self-aligned people are open and easily connected to their own personal source of inspiration and potential. They, therefore, radiate self-love, which in turn invites love back into their world. Their relationships are not drained by need but, instead, fueled by love.

The ultimate truth is that all relationships are not built on a foundation of what others think about you but on what you think about yourself, and if you take a moment to simply listen to what is being reflected back to you through all relationships, there is so much you can learn about yourself.

However, you have to be ready and willing to see and love the reflection, no matter what, for your heart to fully open! You have to be willing to grow into yourself in order to connect fully with the person before you. And no one has the power to choose this for you but yourself.

About the Author

Claire Timmis is a soulfully married mother of three who lives in the Cotswolds, UK. As a channel and a healer, she facilitates self alignment workshops and retreats, both internationally and from her peaceful lakeside lodge in England.

Passionate about the land, and remembering its hidden secrets, she also leads tours of discovery and awakening around British sacred sites.

http://www.clairetimmis.com

THREE SIMPLE PRINCIPLES TO MANIFEST SOULFUL RELATIONSHIPS

Rachel Olliffe

Have you ever wondered why your relationships with others do not fully satisfy your needs? Do you feel that some people create more conflict, confusion, and disruption in your life than you wish? Now is the time to review these relationships and transform them into relationships that reflect the real you, that fulfill your needs and create harmony in your life.

There are three simple principles which will allow you to transform the relationships you currently have and to attract new people into your life that serve to support, nurture, and explore who you truly are in an accepting and loving way. These principles are to love yourself, to treat others as you wish to be treated, and to follow the formula of manifestation to initiate the Universal Law of Attraction.

1. Love Yourself First

First and foremost, you must nurture, love, and accept yourself exactly the way you are. When you love and accept yourself, faults and all, you bring a whole, loving heart to a relationship. Alternatively, if you feel that you are unlovable, unattractive, and undesirable to others, such negative feelings will encourage you to seek other people to fill the void you feel within yourself. Automatically, this creates a dynamic of need in the relationship which, if not fulfilled, will create anxiety and resentment and may lead to conflict. When you change the dynamic of your relationships so that you do not seek others to allay your insecurities, you take control of your own needs and do not demand fulfillment from other people.

By approaching your relationships as a whole-hearted, loving being, you empower yourself to give more of who you are and to seek less to take from others what you should actually bring to the relationship yourself. If you do not approach other people with a sense of need from them, but rather to offer them who you are, your relationships will be more soulful, and less conflict will ensue.

To unconditionally love and accept yourself is not an easy principle to master. A journey of self development, introspection, and life experiences will assist you to learn to love your weaknesses as much as your strengths. When you can look in the mirror and love everything you see, despite your imperfections, your heart will be whole and full of love. Every time you feel like you are unworthy or unattractive, have failed or made a mistake, or have not fulfilled your expectations of yourself, try to remember that you are perfect exactly the way you are in every moment. When you offer yourself this unconditional love you will have the ability to offer unconditional love to others.

Try to accept both the positive and negative aspects of all other people despite how annoying and difficult the personality traits of other people can be. When you acknowledge that all people have imperfections and are deserving of the same love you offer yourself, you will find that your relationships with them will become more meaningful.

2. Treat Others as You Wish to Be Treated

The second principle of manifesting soulful relationships is simply to treat others as you wish and deserve to be treated. This ancient principle is not as easy as it sounds. It requires offering unconditional love and absolute forgiveness. Unconditional love means offering love without the expectation of receiving love in return. It also requires giving love despite other people's annoying habits and even destructive behaviors.

The ultimate challenge lies in offering complete forgiveness for all wrongdoings against you. When other people have hurt or betrayed you or have been angry and aggressive towards you, it is necessary for you to forgive them for their behavior in order for you to create a soulful relationship with them; however, offering forgiveness does not mean that you must accept or tolerate a breach of your boundaries or unacceptable conduct. Rather, you are releasing the burden of carrying the anger, resentment, or hatred that you would otherwise feel about their conduct. If you choose to end a dysfunctional relationship, releasing your negativity toward the other person will not only serve to uplift you, but will also allow you to release them with love.

A person who masters the offering of unconditional love and the forgiveness of wrongdoing will have an open heart that develops deep, loving, committed, and supportive relationships with others. Be it with a partner, child, parent, or co-worker, utilizing these two elements will serve to improve your relationships with these people to a soulful level despite whatever tension or challenges your relationships face. You will not only honor your true, inner self, but you will also respect and honor the true self of the other person.

The offering of unconditional love and forgiveness is the greatest gift you can give yourself and to those around you.

3. The Universal Law of Attraction

The Law of Attraction, put simply, means that like attracts like. In the context of manifesting a soul mate, the type of energy you put out into the Universe will be brought back to you and will be manifested in the world. The formula required for any type of manifestation is:

Thought + Word + Action = Manifestation

The thought which is required for manifestation is intention. And intention is the cornerstone of the Law of Attraction.

Once you set the intention to create something in your life, you set in motion the vital elements required to manifest that which you desire.

First, it is important that your intention be pure and within the divine, highest good of all. Creating a soulful relationship with another person is one of the purest and most divine intentions that exist in this world.

Second, words must be spoken out loud to support your intention. These accompanying words must be in the present tense, as though you now already have what you wish for. A few examples might be:

- "I now have a soulful relationship with my partner."

- "I now have a loving and supportive family."

- "I now have deep and meaningful connections with my friends that are uplifting and fun."

The importance of speaking out loud what you intend to create is often overlooked. It is not enough for the words to be merely spoken as thoughts in your mind. You must speak the words out loud, either to yourself in the form of prayer or to other people in casual conversation. Words have a very strong energetic vibration, which carry within them the power to create. Sound is just another form of energy, and the Universe will respond to that energy by attracting to you that which you have spoken of.

Third, in order to practically create what you desire, you must take action. Without action, there cannot be manifestation. You must do something to further your goal in order for the Universe to respond to your desire. It is not enough, for example, to have the intention to find a soul mate and say out loud to the Universe that "I am now in a loving relationship with my soul mate" only to then sit on the couch and watch TV.

Hope alone will not cause the Universe to create your soul mate to knock on your door. It is important that you also interact with society, whether it is by participating in community services or group recreational activities or via social media or online dating services. These supporting actions create a significant momentum of energy and, according to the Law of Attraction, the Universe will respond by assisting you to manifest a soulful relationship.

The formula for manifestation is the same if you wish to transform a current relationship. You must hold the thought of the intention to transform your relationship into a deeper, more soulful one. You must say out loud, preferably to the other person, your desire to change your relationship with them to become more supportive, loving, accepting, and forgiving. Next, you must carry out actions that support your words, such as listening when they need support, helping when asked, having patience when tested, offering love without expectation, and forgiving when necessary. If you follow the formula for manifestation, the Universal Law of Attraction will respond and you will find that the behavior of the people around you will change.

Conversely, just as like attracts like, opposite intentions repel and cause disharmony. If the other person does not hold the same divine intention to uplift your relationship with them to a soulful level, then it is likely that the relationship will end or will be strictly limited in its nature. At one time or another, all people experience some kind of disharmony in their relationships. These relationships are set to challenge you to be a better person and to acknowledge your part in the interactions within them. They encourage you to accept other people as they are, to identify and improve upon your weaknesses, and to learn how to better deal with such situations in the future. The lesson from these types of relationships is often to be more loving, more accepting, or more forgiving, or to have more self-worth and stricter boundaries of what is acceptable behavior to you. Either way, challenging and dysfunctional relationships can be a blessing in disguise, provided you learn from them so that you do not attract similar relationships in the future.

If you love yourself and do not seek validation from others, treat others as you wish to be treated by offering them unconditional love and forgiveness; and you follow the formula for manifestation, the Universal Law of Attraction will bring to you the soulful relationships you desire. These principles sound easy enough but can be quite hard to master and apply every day.

It is not a matter of luck but of your own soul-searching and your willingness to learn and grow to better yourself. It is important for you to learn to unconditionally love and forgive yourself. It is also essential to have the intent and belief that you not only deserve soulful relationships, but that you will in fact create soulful relationships right now.

You now have the tools to create healthy, fulfilling relationships. It just takes self-reflection, practice, and patience. Check in with yourself on a daily basis and ask, "Have I followed the three principles today?" If you have not, remind yourself that tomorrow is a new day and you will try again until you are successful. If you continue to practice these principles, you will begin to see your entire life transforming. Relationships at work and at home that have been troubled will become smoother and more harmonious. You may choose to end a relationship that does not have a matching divine intention and no longer serves your highest good. However, such relationships will be released with forgiveness, love, and grace. And for those of you seeking a deeper love, someone to cherish and be cherished by, you will attract a love that only a soulful relationship can provide.

It is with these three simple principles that you will empower yourself to not only enrich your life with more meaningful relationships, but to also transform yourself on your path of personal growth and spiritual enlightenment.

About the Author

Rachel has extensive experience in conducting workshops and coaching sessions to help people achieve their personal goals by teaching them to apply the Universal Laws in their lives. She uses guided meditation and energetic healing techniques to raise their consciousness and release their inner power to manifest their dreams.

Rachel produces a blog and podcasts where she communicates the wisdom of the Spiritual Hierarchy across the world. To find out more about Rachel's teachings and her upcoming books, visit her website and follow her on Facebook, Twitter, and Youtube. Rachel lives in Melbourne, Australia, and also consults as a regulatory compliance lawyer.

http://www.rachelolliffe.com

A SOUL NEEDS TO LOVE, LEARN, AND LIVE

Leona D'vaz

When I close my eyes and think about what a soulful relationship means, I envision being content. Not the kind that comes from complacency or believing that one is truly "happy", but one where there is deep resonance within the core of who you are and what you stand for. To me, it means taking the demons that dance in your mind and heart by the hand to one last dance out of your life. Nurturing yourself with the kindest of words, thoughts, and, most importantly, complete joyous acceptance of you. Every nuance, every grand notion, every facet of your being that makes you individual and unique is the key to unlocking that inner peace we all crave so intensely.

When I finally, *finally* reached that point of inner peace—only just recently—I felt satiated by my own authenticity. It's empowering and enables humility to become a dear friend and confidante. My nemesis was my "ego", and the road has been fraught with incredible obstacles. Being engulfed in complete darkness created such intense fear. There were moments when I went right off track and only that minuscule semblance of hope saw me return and continue on.

Each time, it was my passionate spirit that fueled me to strive toward my life's purpose. I believe that we do have souls, we connect with other souls, and we are all here to leave our imprint. Adversity will act like an elixir and will relentlessly tempt you to give up hope, abort your optimism, and spend your days swimming in pity and demise. Writing this chapter was an opportunity for me to open up a small window into my life and share my journey with you thus far. I truly believe creating and embracing a soulful relationship with yourself *first* is where it all begins.

It all starts with family. Mine, was lead by a gypsyesque father who decided that moving seven times before I was twelve was a good idea. He also decided through his uncontrollable alcoholism and aggression that he would subject my mother and I to a home filled with domestic violence for nineteen years. My formative years from five to thirteen were also tainted with sexual abuse. The foundations of love, trust, and family were not laid down for me, and I played out the hurt in my relationships. For the longest time, I engaged in a duplicitous lifestyle; intrinsically shamed and embarrassed, I presented my most superficial and extroverted self to the world. It was a façade honored by receiving a dux of theatre arts in high school—recognition of my successful performance at masking reality.

The truth aches to come out though; it's like a gnawing pain. Dull at first followed by an incessant drill in your mind. I numbed mine with full immersion into a drug addiction and toxic friendships. *What a ride!* It was a seemingly appropriate solution to aid escapism. I have to say, it's taken an unequivocally long time to find and extricate myself from that soul-destroying behavior. Now, in my mid-thirties, I can look back at over thirty years of self-sabotaging and volatile situations and say that I'm here because of three things I continued to feed my soul with: love, learning, and living.

Let's Talk About Love—It Makes the World Go Around

The love from a mother is an unrelenting force. In my scenario, it wasn't enough to prevent my father from executing his will, but it was more than enough to envelope me and keep my small, fragile child's soul filled with hope. Optimism is so critical for harmony in our hearts and minds. My mother told me, "People can do anything to your body, but they can't take your soul." I only understood her sentiments in later years. At that time, I was filled with anger, betrayal, and disassociation. My relationships saw me as the lead actress in a play that was my life. I ached to be loved and nurtured and to trust. My choice in supporting actress was never my strong point. It always ended in tears, restraining orders, and vowing "to never be that person again".

There was one that was different. He let me go to "find myself, resolve my hurt, and become who I needed to be". The breakup was a landmark moment in my life, as I took his advice, sought professional help, and started the journey inwards to make amends with what aggrieved me.

Unconditional love and acceptance from friends has been pivotal in healing. Ever the "people pleaser", I now look for three key qualities in those I entrust: loyalty, genuine intent, and humility. When you find your soul's music sheet, you only need a few key musicians to bring the song to life. For too long I was playing with an orchestra and drowning out my soul map.

Knowledge is Power

My aunt and my mother came from a long line of teachers and instilled in me a strong affinity with learning. Hand on heart, enriching your mind is one of the best presents you can give yourself. Not only does knowledge help to empower and evolve people, but it also bridges the global divide between "us and them", "poor and rich", "weak and strong". Education saves people and it saved me. Not for one moment since I entered kindergarten have I not been learning. It's my greatest joy and, in moments of solace, the companion that wants me to be the highest version of myself. It wants to be yours too.

My father refused to pay for my high school once I turned fifteen. I remember my mother fighting for me to get a part-time job and I was an employee at a local deli at fourteen and nine months. It was liberating. My aunt paid for my high school and, at that point, I vowed that my life's purpose would be lived. No matter your own personal adversity, you have my full heartfelt support and to learn as much as you need to live your soul's purpose.

We all have a story, and it is my genuine desire to give everyone a voice, we all deserve and need that. I didn't speak out until my mid-twenties, for fear of vocalizing what happened would result in my mother being harmed. Now, I hope my story will strike a chord with anyone who has experienced a similar life. It wasn't until then, that I realized I wasn't alone—a lot of people experienced this behind closed doors and becoming a "lost soul" can happen all too quickly.

The Soul is Inquisitive and Curious

Be courageous and feed it with experiences that are enriching! Life, really, is to be lived. Even though my inner battles continued waging war, I've launched myself into my "passions at the time" headfirst. People used to call me "impulsive" and "the extremist". Or they used to say, "What's she up to now?"

For me, the drive to do the "what I loved" part always far outweighed the "how to do it" one. Ending the relationship with my father was a cornerstone moment for this. It's been almost ten years since we've had contact. The letter I penned him explained my need to move on with my life, irrespective of whether he ever apologized or felt remorse for his actions or not. I expressed that I wished him the clarity to see the error of his actions, feel empathy, and move toward making himself a compassionate human being. It was a cathartic and necessary action for me. At some point, we will sit face to face and draw closure. For now, my focus is on strengthening myself spiritually, mentally, and emotionally (and physically!) so that my soul, heart, and mind are in alignment.

Our world is incredibly "yang" and being introspective and "yin" is of great importance for our own equilibrium.

A Soul Needs to Love, Learn, and Live

Even though our souls have individual journeys, we all intertwine. Through our relationships with each other and ourselves we enhance our purpose and find our soul mates. These are the people who will bring the essence of who we are to the core.

It's my life's dream to gradually help empower abuse victims, and if you are one of them, *you can make it.*

Be ever kind to yourself and seek only authenticity. Feel brave to live the fullest version of yourself.

> *"The ordinary man is the curse of civilization."*
> – The Collector (John Fowles).

About the Author

Leona D'vaz is a marketing manager in the writing industry. A freelance writer, her passion is uncovering people's biographies and life's journeys to bring them to life in the various publications she freelances for.

With a degree in human resource management, she is currently working toward a degree in communications, with a focus on journalism and film. Her developing work as a photojournalist is moving her towards producing documentaries in developing countries and giving our world's under-privileged a voice and a platform for other people to learn and help empower them.

Leona's work and her journey can be followed at her website.

http://www.leonadevaz.com

SURROUNDING YOURSELF
WITH GREATNESS

Sinive Seely

Soulful relationships are the relationships that matter most to us as human beings. They are about the people with whom we share a deep connection: those who allow us to be ourselves and with whom we share our worries, strengths, and dreams. They are those who see the best in us, walk alongside us, hold us up when we fall down, and help us to become better by simply being in their presence. Soulful relationships are all about surrounding yourself with greatness—with those people who will lift you higher than you ever thought possible. They are also about releasing those people who no longer serve you so that you are free to "be" and show up in the world as the most authentic and powerful version of yourself.

People who see, hear, and understand us with their hearts and minds are kindred spirits. I've been gathering a community of these like-minded people in my life for years now. People I call "my tribe." And it is something I recommend you do as well. . . .

Lesson One: Look for soulful connections with those you are destined to meet

When I was thirteen years old, I moved with my family from Auckland, New Zealand, to Peace River, Canada: a small town in northern Alberta with long-cold winters and summer nights that went on forever. My neighbors had also moved to Peace River around the same time as we did. They were from Singapore and had two teenage daughters about my age. I remember watching them from my window and giggling about how silly I thought they looked as they walked shielding themselves from the sun's bright glare with their parasol umbrellas.

Imagine my surprise when these young women soon became my close friends. We bonded over hamburgers and milkshakes, working at the local fast food restaurant while adjusting to the culture shock of living in a totally different world. On the surface, we had nothing in common. We had been raised in completely different cultures, with different customs, beliefs, and values. We had different accents, dressed differently, and really didn't fit in at school. By the time high school ended, we were the best of friends and couldn't help but feel that we had been destined to meet from opposite ends of the globe in this small northern Alberta town.

Today, as adults, we laugh about how girls from New Zealand and Singapore came to be living in Peace River at that time in our lives. And even though we live in different parts of North America and do not see each other often, we know that we share a soulful connection that transcends geography.

Lesson Two: Love those who see you for who you really are

My soon-to-be husband and I met during my first year of university at a church dance. Rather than awkwardly slow-dancing a bible's distance apart, we sat and talked for hours. He was *not* my type. He was shy, reserved, and much shorter than any guy I'd ever dated before. Yet, there was something about him that immediately put me at ease and made me feel slightly giddy. I knew we were destined to be together on our first date when he reached over and held my hand and was so nervous I felt him shaking. Four years later, we were married, and today we have two beautiful daughters and have experienced many adventures together.

My husband is part of my tribe as he has always seen the best in me. When I share my crazy beautiful dreams with him, he lets them linger. He encourages me to follow my heart and wants more than anything for me to be happy. He sees me for who I am and loves me for it. I truly believe this is all any of us want in life: to be seen, heard and understood . . . and most of all, to be loved.

Lesson Three: Be willing to take risks

In 2007 I was inspired to begin a journey of transformation that forever changed the way I saw myself and my life. At the time, I had all the material trappings of success; yet, somehow, I still felt something was missing. I began to ask myself, "Is there more to life than this?"

I remember staring out the window into the dark snowy winter's night and remembering my childhood spent at the beach in New Zealand. It had been twenty years since I had lived there and I found myself longing to return to my homeland. I knew I wanted to move back and experience life there again but was terrified of making such a drastic move with my family. Deep down, I knew it was a risk I had to take. Within a year, I had left my job, sold my house, and moved my family across the world.

Going back to New Zealand was like coming home for me. As I saw my daughters at the beach where I grew up playing in the sand and climbing the same tree I used to climb as a child, I knew that this was exactly where I was meant to be. It felt like my past, present, and future were all aligning to bring this amazing experience to life for me.

In New Zealand I felt an instant connection to the Polynesian people. Being of Samoan Canadian descent, it was an amazing experience to see other people who looked like me, who shared my sense of humor, and who understood and practiced the cultural customs and traditions I had been raised with. The thick Kiwi accent was like music to my ears, and I experienced a sense of belonging like none I had ever felt before in my life.

The literal definition of a tribe is a group who share common ancestry and culture. In New Zealand, I found my roots—my connection to my tribe through my past, present, and future.

Lesson Four: Surround yourself with greatness

Oprah Winfrey said it best when she said, "Surround yourself only with people who are going to take you higher." I didn't fully understand what this meant until late last year when I signed up to take an executive coaching course. I had always been interested in coaching, but it had been a long time since I'd been in university and the thought of returning after so many years was daunting. As I read over the biographies of the other students, I soon learned that my class was full of over-achievers: the CEO of a major Canadian organization, an Olympic athlete, senior executives, seasoned business people, entrepreneurs, academics, mountain climbers, and social climbers. And then there was me.

At the time, I was a mid-career professional working in a job I enjoyed but one that certainly didn't hold the same bragging rights. I felt small and insignificant. It was overwhelming introducing myself to this group of amazing people. I had no idea what I had to offer this group. All I knew was that I was passionate about coaching and that I needed to be there among them. In order to succeed, I'd have to face my fears. If that meant being around some of the best and brightest people I'd ever met, I was willing to walk that path.

During the eight months I was in the program, I formed some deep connections with the members of my program. We were all on the same journey together baring our souls as we did the personal groundwork required to become exceptional coaches. Through this experience I learned that as human beings we are all the same. We may look different on the outside, but inside we all share fears, hopes, and dreams, regardless of our job title or position in life.

Today, I consider my coaching colleagues some of my greatest advocates, supporters, and cheerleaders. They are indeed my tribe, and I now see my own greatness reflected through their eyes.

Lesson Five: Find your cheerleaders

When I decided to quit my job to follow my passion and start my own business, I was surprised at how my decision elicited varying responses from my friends and family. Some were very supportive and excited for me, others were cautiously optimistic, and then there were some who totally fell by the wayside that I lost contact with.

I learned very quickly that in order to succeed, I not only needed to surround myself with greatness, but I also had to find my cheerleaders. Those people who were there on the sidelines watching both my successes and failures and cheering me on through it all. My cheerleaders were there because they *wanted* to be, and their optimism, energy, and positivity spurred me on during the hard times and inevitable bumps along the road.

One particular young woman comes to mind when I think of my cheerleaders. She exudes passion, excitement, and energy on my behalf. When I begin to doubt myself she holds up a mirror to allow me to see who I really am and what I have to offer the world. She believes in me and what I am doing no matter the obstacles and always has a kind word of support to offer. It's largely because of her that I have been able to grasp onto my dreams and hold tight. I will forever be grateful for her love and support. She is my number one cheerleader and will always hold a special place in my tribe.

Lesson Six: Release those who no longer serve you

We all have people in our life who are toxic. They drain our energy because they just take, take and then take some more. Sometimes they wear a mask so it's difficult to determine whether they're our friends or foes. They smile to your face all the while behaving in a way that leaves you feeling unsettled.

Maya Angelou has said, "People will forget what you said, people will forget what you did, but people will never forget how you made them feel." How you feel when you are around someone is a good indication of whether they deserve to be in your life or not.

In my own life I've had to release some toxic relationships in order to move forward. I do not hold grudges or wish ill on them, I just know when the relationship is no longer serving me and ensure that I surround myself with people who will lift me higher. There is no room in a tribe for toxic people. Release them to create the space for you to be your best self.

Lesson Seven: Be open to the possibilities; show up as the most authentic and powerful version of yourself!

The final lesson I learned in finding my tribe was to be open to possibilities. Manifesting is about being open to creating in life what it is you most desire. In order to do this you must show up as the most authentic and powerful version of yourself. By surrounding yourself with greatness you tap into your place of possibility. You attract those people into your life whom will inspire you to do and to be better.

Building a tribe takes time. You must be open to making yourself vulnerable, to doing the work and to being your best self. Each and every one of us has a tribe of people who will accept us as we are and see the best in us. We just have to find them! I invite you today to find your own tribe, to surround yourself with greatness and to show up in the world as your best self.

About the Author

Sinive Seely is a certified executive coach, professional speaker, and corporate trainer. Sinive has lived and worked in both New Zealand and Canada, and she owns and operates her own business, Sinive Seely Coaching and Consulting. Sinive is passionate about coaching women leaders to live inspired lives on purpose. She helps people connect to their Passion, Purpose, Potential, Possibility, and Power!

http://www.siniveseely.com

ANYTHING IS POSSIBLE!

Jen Hannah

"Where is he?" I asked aloud. "We have work to do!" It was three years ago in October, and I had long known that the man I would choose as my partner in life would be someone with whom I shared a mission. Family would be a part of that mission, absolutely; I desired to share the sacred calling of parenting with him.

And even more.

For as long as I can remember, I've known that life is about more than just working a meaningless job and then *maybe* having the energy at the end of the day to do what we truly love. Granted, the "how" has oftentimes eluded me, though from my very core I've longed for that something "more". A big part of my Dream has always been to encourage and inspire others to live *their* Dreams. My belief runs deep that when we are using the gifts and passions we've been given, and when we are *being* who we truly are, we can't help but make a difference in the world around us. The man of my Dreams would believe that, too, I knew. He would be passionate about living his *own* passions, and together we would empower others on the journey to *their* Dreams.

My fervent conviction in the importance of Dreams had led me to a life somewhat outside the box. I'd tried the nine-to-five thing. It just didn't fit. Then, in my early twenties, I was told about The Passion Test: a process that supports a person in clearly identifying their top passions. After all, how is one to *live* their Dreams if those Dreams aren't clearly known?

Every few months, I'd sit down and redo my Passion Test. Regularly revisiting it helped bring my priorities into focus and, regardless of how many times I repeated this powerful process, a few key things kept showing up. Though the order or wording sometimes shifted slightly, it soon became clear that in my ideal life, I was a) living my passions/sharing my gifts with the world; b) empowering people around the world to live their Dreams; and c) experiencing a deeply spiritual and purpose-filled relationship with the man of my dreams.

This level of clarity gifted me with the awareness and courage to act on opportunities that were in alignment with my passions, and, with peace of mind, to decline those that would divert me from my true calling. So when the opportunity came to be certified as a Passion Test Facilitator, I jumped on it! When the prospect arose to both perform and record some of my songs, I said, "Yes!" When *Up With People* confirmed that they had a few remaining openings for a six-month worldwide tour doing music performance and volunteer work, I signed up! How could I pass up an opportunity to share my love for music *and* to deepen my sense of global citizenship through serving in communities around the world?

Another opportunity came in the summer, mere months prior to my declared "Where is he? We have work to do!" My Passion Test mentor, Cheryl, told me about an upcoming Volun-Tour trip to Vietnam that she was going on. Jana Stanfield, one of the top artists in the Positive Music world, would be leading the trip. The group would be spending time in orphanages and schools, bringing hope and joy to the lives of hundreds of children. Hmm . . . I'd get to experience yet another new-to-me culture, make a real difference in the lives of children, *and* get to spend time with a woman who was successfully living *her* Dream of sharing her inspiring music worldwide. This opportunity was congruent with many of my core passions, so I took the leap!

A couple of months after signing up and writing the cheque, I lost my job.

"What now?" I wondered. "How can I realistically take this trip? It would be totally irresponsible to go, considering I don't even know how I'll be paying my bills next month!"

That's when a dear friend and fellow Dreamer suggested that the financial part would be a non-issue compared to what I would gain by going. In an exquisite moment of foreshadowing, she intuited that this trip would be "life-changing." Man, I had no idea.

As I saw the externals of my life changing, I knew that space was being created for me to dive more fully into my Dreams. It was time. Through my fear and countless questions—But how do I. . .? What if. . .? Can this possibly. . .?—I stated my intention that once my employment insurance ran out, I would never work a "job" again. My income would come solely from living my passions. To get super clear on what I desired, I did another Passion Test. The results? Written three years ago, on October 26:

"When my life is ideal, I am . . .

1) Trusting and going with the Flow of Life

2) Lovingly giving my gifts to the world

3) An integral part of a passionate and conscious team that inspires people around the world to live their Dreams

4) Joyfully living the Adventure of Life in partnership with the man of my Dreams

5) Spending my time as I choose, doing the things I love."

I then created three vision boards to flesh out my intentions. One board I filled with all the things that made me bubble over with joy. On another, I wrote out what I wanted to *say* with my life—my messages. And the third I filled with all the attributes I could think of that I desired in my life partner: everything from "soul-seeker" and "older than me" to "Dreamer" and "loves traveling". I got specific. Being keenly aware of the great openness that Change had been gifted to me, I held out my desires, released them to the Author of Dreams, and, with a smile, declared, "Where is he? We have work to do!"

The following month, on November 27, I walked into the waiting area for flight CI0007 at LAX to meet the people I'd be traveling to Vietnam with. And . . . there he was.

I didn't know it right away, but there he was, the man of my Dreams—the Bubble Man.

Prior to the trip, we'd received an information packet that included the names and a brief description of each of our fellow travelers. Upon reading that there would be a guy in our group who performed bubble shows, I'd thought, "Neat. Bubbles are pretty cool. The kids in the orphanages and schools that we'll be visiting will enjoy that." Little did I know. . . .

On the third night of our twelve-day trip, while floating through Halong Bay aboard the beautiful *Victory*, our group held a "No Talent Required Show". I signed up to sing my song, *Grateful*. A couple hours before the event, I got cold feet. Not because I was nervous to sing in front of my fellow travelers, but because of a rogue thought that darted into my mind from thin air: "If he hears me sing, he'll fall in love with me."

Whoa! What?! That's slightly narcissistic, isn't it?! But there it was.

Yes, I'd been impressed by the Bubble Dude's kindness and the few bubble tricks I'd seen up to that point, but, truly, I wasn't sure if I wanted to open the "feelings" door with him. He lived in the US; I lived in Canada. He was several years older than me. He wore a lot of purple. Sure, I thought he'd make a great friend, but I didn't foresee anything beyond that. I hated the thought of inadvertently encouraging his interest and him getting hurt. My decision was made: I wouldn't sing that night. And then yet another—*stronger*—thought rose unbidden: *You've been given a gift that is to be shared. Who are you to withhold it?*

So I sang.

The next morning, the Bubble Guy and I chatted over breakfast. He asked about my process for songwriting; I told him it's usually lyrics first. I asked about his bubble show; he told me that it's more than just bubble tricks—it has a message. He asked if anyone had ever commissioned a song from me; I replied, "Yes, a few times." I asked about the message of his show; he said that he uses the bubble tricks to encourage kids to believe in their Dreams and be persistent in following them because anything is possible. . . . (Remember that "feelings" door? In that moment, it opened just a crack.) He asked if I'd write a theme song for his *Bubble Wonders* show; I said, "Yes."

A few days later, Cheryl and I were asked to lead the group through The Passion Test. Between addressing the group and explaining the different parts of the process, she and I would offer support one-on-one. Guiding people as they gain clarity on their top passions is such a privilege and leads to a much deeper level of interpersonal connection. And I *was* a bit curious… what did Bubble Boy's ideal life look like? Again, my rational mind whispered for me to leave it alone. So when he requested individual assistance with his Passion Test, I let Cheryl go to him.

During the remaining week of the trip, Mr. Bubble and I enjoyed each other's company and several more heartfelt conversations. The door in my heart continued to inch open with each interaction we shared. On the final night, our group members had another opportunity to share—a song, dance, poem, or whatever. Again, I sang. The Bubble Guru presented a portion of his show that tells of his Dream to create something seemingly impossible. And this time, it was *his* turn to completely capture *my* heart with what he shared—a square bubble and the words: "What's *your* Dream? What impossible things are *you* going to do? What's *your* square bubble? Just remember, no matter your age or situation, all you have to remember and believe are three simple words: anything is possible."

The door of my heart flew open. There he was! My *partner*! The one I'd been waiting for! He was *already* living his passion, and he was encouraging people around the world to believe in *their* Dreams! He'd offered to do whatever he could to support my Dream of sharing my positive music! *And* he was going to *pay* me to write a song for *Bubble Wonders* with the very message I felt that I was born to tell!

Yet there remained a part of me that didn't know if I was ready to lay my heart on the line. There were too many unknowns, too many obstacles that we would potentially have to face. But there remained one thing that I had to know: did he even *want* to be in a relationship? Was that in his top passions? If so, what was he looking for in a partner? Did I even remotely fit the bill?

It was clear that a bit of reconnaissance was in order, so I recruited Cheryl. Yes, it's true! The Mission: find out if a relationship was a part of the Bubble Maestro's ideal life. The Hurdle: the trip was essentially over. Our group was bound for the airport that morning. At the final possible moment, Cheryl came to me. Mission accomplished. The final word? Yes! This blessed Bubble Man did envision a life with someone special. And my brand of special did, indeed, fit the bill.

Our story, when told in full, holds many more moments of magic and synchronicity, though for now I'll just say that a few months later, Geoff Akins and I officially became partners for life. Fast forward another few months, and my first full-length album, *Grateful*, was released, featuring the *Bubble Wonders'* theme song, *Anything Is Possible*. Half a year following that, my beloved Bubs was by my side—and our babe was growing within my womb!—as I took the stage and *Anything Is Possible* was named winner of a Posi Music Award!

Yes, Dreams *do* come true, and *anything* truly *is possible!*

About the Author

Jen Hannah is an award-winning songwriter, singer and (unabashed) dreamer who believes in living with purpose and passion, in living love and loving life. She sings her soul's song, and people around the globe have been impacted by her positive music.

Authors, coaches, personal development gurus, and (her favorite!) the Bubble Wonders show have enriched their brands with Jen's custom songs.

Jen also uses The Passion Test and her writing to offer inspiration and the opportunity for others to join her in the belief that when it comes to our deepest Dreams, anything is possible!

http://www.jenhannahsings.com/

I AM THE ARTIST OF MY LIFE

Leanne Watson

Do you remember that defining moment when you were a kid and you knew in your heart and soul what you wanted to be when you grow up? For me, this happened when I was fifteen, when my parents took me to see the musical theater production of *Joseph and the Amazing Technicolor Dreamcoat*. I was sitting in the audience, watching the actors on stage and thought to myself, "That is what I want to be when I grow up." I wanted to be on stage; I wanted to impact people's lives in a positive way. But the direction my life took after I finished high school was very different from my childhood dream.

My first year out of high school, my mum was diagnosed with cancer. The doctors gave her six months to live, and in six months she was gone. I could use my mum's death as the reason I lost sight of my dream to be on stage; but, to be honest, I lost sight of my dream somewhere in my final years of high school. I didn't realize at the time that I was subconsciously carrying a belief about myself that I was not worth the effort, so my attempts to pursue a life on stage were mediocre at best. This belief was created at a very young age from a string of childhood experiences (and a story for another time).

Throughout my twenties I went from job to job, hoping to find a substitute dream that I could pursue. By my late twenties, I had found some direction when I started working in human resources (HR). For eight years I worked in corporate HR, specializing in employment law. In addition to being on stage, I was also passionate about helping people, which is why HR seemed to be a good "Plan B". I also enrolled in a part time bachelor's degree in business, majoring in HR—even though I hated studying and was never very academic at school.

Working in HR and studying at university were the complete opposite to what I wanted to do with my life. During my eight years in HR, I changed jobs eight times and every bad day at work ended with me practically in tears, complaining to my husband that this was not what I wanted to do with my life.

2008 was a particularly stressful time: I was working in a demanding, unhealthy environment and was two years into my degree, which felt like a ball and chain around my neck. I desperately needed some creativity in my life—so, on a whim, I signed up to an acting course at a local theater in Sydney. A couple of courses later, I had the opportunity to audition for a play and I landed a part. I couldn't have been happier. Being on stage again was magical, and I knew that I wanted more.

In 2010 I eventually took a leap of faith, moved to a part time HR position, enrolled in a part time acting course, and took up additional subjects at university to speed up my degree. In 2011 I spent three months in New York, further developing my skills as an actor. Living in New York was the turning point. I felt like my dream of being on stage could actually become a reality, and the thought of going back to a desk job and continuing with my degree was *far* from appealing. I guess the Universe agreed, as by mid-2011 my life went in a direction that completely ripped apart everything I knew and challenged everything I believed.

My husband and I were not spending much time together, mainly because I kept myself so busy to prevent the truth of my life from catching up with me. I was extremely unhappy and stressed with work and university, and I realized that working in HR was not helping the people that needed it the most. Plus, I wanted to focus more of my time on acting.

It felt like my whole life was falling apart—like I was one of those snow dome souvenirs and all the pieces of my life had been tossed into the air waiting to see if or when they would settle. I kept asking myself why I wasn't happy. On paper, I ticked all the boxes: I was married to a wonderful man, I had a great corporate job with a six-figure salary and was on my way to completing my degree, I lived in a beautiful house and had a great wardrobe, and I traveled regularly. And all I thought of was how I would give it all up if I could be on stage every minute of my life. I was lost, angry, and needed guidance.

The guidance I was searching for came from a new colleague, whom I believe was meant to come into my life at that exact moment. I shared with her that all I ever wanted to do was be on stage and use acting as a platform to drive social change but was unsure which direction to take. My colleague recommended an amazing book that changed my life called *Half the Sky*. The book focuses on stories of sex trafficking, maternal mortality, sexual violence, microfinance, and girls' education. After reading this book I knew this was the area I wanted to help in. I wanted to help women and children who are denied an education and treated inhumanely simply because they are female. I wanted to give them the opportunity to live the life of their dreams regardless of their beginnings.

But to do this, I knew I had to stand up and fight for myself first. How could I be a strong role model for these women when I was hiding behind my own fears? It was at that point that I thought to myself, "Mum was forty-six when she died." I was thirty-six at the time. "If I knew I had ten years left of my life, would I continue to sit at this desk staring at this computer?" I did not want to get to the end of my life with a list of regrets. It was time to get out of my head and let my heart guide me, but how the hell was I going to do this? Where was I to start?

I started by questioning everything: my beliefs and way of thinking. By talking openly about what was going on in my life, I opened myself up to allow the right information to come in, which would then guide me through what was an extremely emotional, but rewarding, journey—physically, mentally, and spiritually.

I met with a kinesiologist/life-coach who changed my world in more ways than I could ever imagine. With her help, I cleared a lot of old baggage and confronted my fears and insecurities. She helped me understand that the people and experiences in my life were a mirror reflection of how I felt about myself. She enlightened me to the awareness that I am not my thoughts and feelings and that I needed to take responsibility for my choices to be able to move out of the past and create a different future for myself.

In addition to my kinesiology sessions, I started meditating and reading books and blogs on spirituality, self-development, metaphysics, and philosophy. I saw a tantric healer and a medium and started to talk openly things I had always felt ashamed of. I surrounded myself with people who were in alignment with the highest ideals of myself and filled my world with positive and inspiring stories, quotes, and affirmations. I had lived most of my life with negative affirmations, so I decided it was time to learn to love myself unconditionally and live my life fearlessly.

I knew I was on the right path because it felt right in my gut and my world began to change in a positive way. People and opportunities that were in alignment with my dreams and desires came into my life. I developed deeper connections with friends and family. I felt lighter and present and had an energy and love for myself that I had never felt before. It was at this point that I knew the only person standing in my way was me—and if I was successful in a career that was not my passion, imagine just how successful I would be doing what I loved.

So, finally, with this newfound belief in myself, I quit my HR job, took a leave of absence from university, and separated from my husband. I spent seven months traveling the globe, volunteering with children from vulnerable backgrounds in Cambodia and India, and studying Shakespeare at the Royal Academy of Dramatic Art in London.

A year later, I signed with an amazing agent, went back to university to finish my degree—but on my own terms—and spent two months in Los Angeles and New York continuing to develop my acting skills. Since then, I have performed in a play and have been offered a role in a Shakespeare production. Additionally, I am creating a photo book of my travels to raise money for the organizations I volunteered at in Cambodia and India, and I have had the opportunity to share my story, thanks to Älska Publishing.

My journey was more than I could have ever imagined and, although I am now in a better place, there were many challenges that I had to overcome. The hardest part of the whole journey was walking away from someone I care deeply about and whom I knew still really loved me. However, I knew I had to do this for myself. I had always given so much to the people I cared about that I had completely forgot about myself; it was time to choose *me*. Another challenge was learning to let go and trust that everything was happening perfectly, even though I didn't have all the answers. Additionally, moving through the emotions and letting go of my old ways of thinking and the long-held beliefs about myself took some time and dedication.

I overcame the challenges of my journey by being completely open to all of life's lessons and experiences along the way. My greatest lessons were that it is *okay* to choose me and that I have the power to change my life by changing my attitude of mind. My greatest experience was reaching a place of unconditional love and acceptance for myself.

One thing I noticed while on my journey was that, by following my dreams, I inspired the people around me to start following theirs. I shared everything that I learned along the way but allowed my friends to take what resonated with them and find their own path. Living life as a conscious human being is such a peaceful and rewarding way to be, and the great thing is that anyone can do it. All they need to do is start taking steps in the right direction, be completely honest with themselves, back themselves 110 percent, and learn to love themselves wholeheartedly.

Everyone can have the life of their dreams if they really want to. Time is precious, so don't waste time trying to live your life for someone else. What people say and do is a projection of their own internal struggle; it has nothing to do with you, so be Teflon—let criticism and judgment slide off you—and go out and live your life fearlessly.

As for what is next for me, I will continue to pursue my dreams wholeheartedly and be open to all the amazing experiences that life has to offer. Additionally, as I build my profile as an actor, I will continue to raise awareness in the areas I am so passionate about and hopefully inspire others to follow their dreams. And I will continue to wake up every morning with the belief that something wonderful is possible today.

About the Author

Leanne Watson is an actor and humanitarian and the artist of her life. Raised in Sydney, Australia, she loves the theater, yoga, her vintage bicycle, and exploring the world. She is passionate about living the life of her dreams and is an inspiring light who seeks to empower others to follow their dreams as well. Her energy, passion, and witty sense of humor attract the most wonderful people into her life.

Leanne absolutely thrives when on stage or giving back to the causes she is passionate about—whether it is through volunteering or creating ways to raise money.

http://www.leannewatson.tumblr.com

LOST AND FOUND

Tarra Bennett

The Sign says: *Lost and Found: Lost Stress and Found Peace on this trip to Soulful Relationships. This four-day outdoor experiential workshop teaches you to achieve, enjoy, and maintain soulful relationships.*

Those words speak to me. They sound exactly like something that I'm looking for, and in this moment I decide to take the trip.

Day 1: Destination: Soulful Relationship!

My bags are packed, and I am off with my knapsack on my back and with my comfortable orange rubber boots. I am cozy in my warm, hot pink waterproof attire. The rest of the group, twelve in all, seems to be as at ease as I am.

Four hours of hiking and we arrive at our site. The terrain on the trail is grassy and smooth with flowers galore, rolling green hills, a thin forest, butterflies, and a pine scent in the air. Heaven!

I awaken to the beautiful sound of birds chirping. I feel happy and totally at peace. It's 7 a.m., and I can hear people moving around outside. I can feel that it's time to get out of bed.

Our guide welcomes us and shares what is expected for today: "We dedicate today to being mindful of our habits, our grievances, and our judgments. As we observe these thoughts, we bring them to the place in our mind that is peaceful. We see past the mistaken idea of "what we think we are" to the truth of "Only Love will bring us peace." We see past the judgments to only the good in each other. We want to remember the Love we are. We want to remember that we are all safe when Love is present.

You have meditation, yoga, nature walk, bird-watching, lunch, and dinner posted in your itinerary. During this time, notice and record all the judgments you experience yourself having of each participant in the group, including judgments about yourself."

As the day passes, I notice that I'm pleasant and sociable with everyone but surprised by how, on the inside, I have judgments. I notice that my thoughts are not always in line with my facial expression. At times, I have a smile on my face, while inside I'm thinking that this person is helpless, a jerk, too old, too fat, too slim, too argumentative . . . the list goes on. I become aware that it happens all the time in my daily life, but it somehow feels normal, as if this is our natural state of being.

I record, as best I can, my uncensored thoughts of each person.

The judgments are in.

As I get ready to retire for the evening, I reflect now on the possible consequences of this entire dynamic of judging one another? It leads to the impossible problem of separation and valuation. Everyone becomes "appraised" as to their worth, me included.

I think about how my day would be if all my thoughts of everyone were neutral. If I had no judgments and could just see past the face, the personality, the cloths, the hair or lack of, the color of the skin, etc. and see through to the core, which is innocence and love. Peaceful!

It occurs to me that it is my interpretation of what I am seeing that is creating all this havoc in my mind. It has nothing to do with what is the truth underneath all the rubble of my mind. If I could just accept everyone at face value, I wouldn't get tripped up. If I could view my day the way I view reading a book and just accept that it is how it is. The sky is blue; the person is talking fast; the river flows. I would not make it wrong for flowing more today than yesterday. I would be much more peaceful. I wouldn't think that the sky is wrong for shining blue nor would I think that there is something wrong if someone was talking fast or slow. If I could see everything as neutral I would be at peace. Like the kid in the sand box playing, peaceful.

It's getting late; I will have a quick meditation to set the tone for a good night's sleep.

Day 2:

I arrive late for the group session. Our guide has instructed us to get into pairs and share our judgments from yesterday. Unfortunately, most of the pairing off has already occurred by the time I arrive.

My partner is Jess. I'm a little embarrassed to share my judgments, so I'm hoping that she will go first. However, before I am able to get the words out of my mouth, she says, "Do you mind if I go second?"

"No, that's fine," I respond. I feel sheepish and awkward as I get started. I go through all of my judgments about myself and say that I am sorry after each one. She listens as if each judgment is about her and appreciates it when I say that I am sorry.

Finally, I get to my judgments about her. I sheepishly say, "I thought that you were so big you might have to roll rather then walk to get around." I immediately say, "I am so sorry," but she just looks at me in stunned disbelief. She wants to speak, but all she can do is cry. I just sit there staring at her, feeling very embarrassed. Finally, I can't take it anymore, so I, too, start to cry. I say through my tears, "I want to give up this habit of judging others. I see how hurtful it can be."

She stops crying, looks at me, and responds with "I forgive you." Then, after a short pause, "I too want to stop judging others. Wait till you hear what I thought when I saw you."

We both took a deep breath and a sip of water before she started to work through her judgments. She got to me last and says that she immediately disliked me for being physically slim and beautiful and thought I must be very, *very* shallow. I see now how wrong I was. She then says, "I am so sorry. Will you forgive me?"

I respond with "Yes."

We thank each other, hug, and hold hands for a moment. I feel a deep sense of gratitude between us, as if we both really got how it's our own defenses that is driving this whole judging game.

As the group loosened up and got to know each other, it became clear how off the mark our judgments were. By the end of the day, we all felt equally committed to the challenge of a lifetime: committing to become conscious of our judgments of others and to willingly file all judgments under mistaken perceptions.

Day 3:

Our guide starts off day 3 by saying, "Today, we choose to be happy, which means that today we choose to forgive. Forgiveness is the key to happiness and we want you to turn forgiveness into a habit. Do it daily. Hourly, even. Forgive anytime you feel inside that you were out of line in a conversation or anytime someone else says something that you resent or angers you. Over time, your forgiveness will become natural and the results immeasurable.

Now, here's a forgiveness process you can follow to help you forgive someone whom you think has hurt you. You can apply this process to everyone you need to forgive including yourself:

First choose the person you want to forgive—the "enemy". Now think of a friend or someone you trust and love. Close your eyes. Visualize the "enemy". Look at them for a while. Perceive some light in them— a little gleam which you had never noticed. Find some little spark of brightness shining through the ugly picture that you hold of them (use a flashlight inside of them if you are having trouble).

Now, see the light somewhere within them, and now let this light extend until it covers them and makes the picture beautiful. View this changed beautiful perception for a while...Now turn your mind to one you call a friend. Transfer the light you learned to see around your former "enemy" to your friend. . . . Now see the light that was transferred to your friend, notice how they feel as more than a friend to you, for in that light is their holiness and yours.

Now let your friend offer you the light you saw in them. Now let your former "enemy" and your friend unite in blessing you.

You join them in a circle, and feel your oneness.

God bless!"

I work the process on everyone whom I think I need to forgive. The most difficult one is my third grade teacher who has asked me to stand up in front of the class and answer a problem that was on the board. However, since I haven't done my homework, I didn't know the correct answer. Upon hearing my incorrect answer, she ran down the aisle to where I was standing, slapped me, and I've hated her ever since.

After seeing the light in her, during the forgiveness process, I realized it wasn't the slap that hurt, it was the embarrassment and shame I felt for not knowing the answer. I realize all I had to do was use my voice when asked the question and say, "I am sorry, Ms. Follett. My Mom was sick and I didn't have anyone to help me with my homework." I began to realize how much I cherished my hate for her. Even after all these years, I still wanted to hang onto hating her. In a way, it felt good to hate her. I stored that anger for many years. Science tells us stored anger creates blockages that, in turn, create illnesses in the body.

I become aware that as we let Love bring Light to unforgiving thoughts, we make way for the joy of being as Love created us. I come to realize that it's not what someone does or says to you that hurts you; it's how you interpret the situation that really hurts.

Day 4:

There is a fresh scent of summer in the air as the final day begins. Our guide simply asks us to share our experiences and comments on the weekend.

I say, "Something interesting happened to me as I went through the forgiveness process. I realized that none of the people I forgave had actually hurt me, even my worst offender hadn't hurt me. It was only my own interpretation of the event that hurt me. I created the hurt myself with my misperception.

I have come to realize that without a misperceived judgment there would be no attack on anyone. If we could have the presence of mind to step back and reflect on the situation and know if we feel to attack anyone it is only our own judgment of the situation we are responding to.

If I change my mind, I change my thoughts. If I change my thoughts, I change my actions. Imagine if you can: no attack, no wars—on the home front or on battlefields.

I get it. I am to take full responsibility for everything that happens to me in my life.

All comments are in.

The guide reminds to:

1: Be mindful of our habit of judging others.

2: Make a habit daily of saying "I am sorry."

3: Make a habit daily of saying "I forgive you."

Remember that it's like bathing: you feel better if you do it daily.

As Mother Teresa said: "I have found the paradox, that if you love until it hurts, there can be no more hurt, only more love."

With Love and Gratitude,

Tarra

About the Author

Tarra Bennett is the founder of the School of Forgiveness dedicated to healing the mind/body through finding the light within. She is a Pathways of Light Ordained Minister, Accessing Inner Wisdom Counselor, and Relationship Enhancement Counselor. She is also a Journey Practitioner, NLP Practitioner, and Dowsing Practitioner and has studied meditation at the International Meditation Institute in India.

http://www.healingfromwithin.ca

THE DEATH OF ME:
A BARDO JOURNEY INTO REBIRTH

Stephanie Lin

I remember when the whisper of death first crept up to my door. It began in the fall of 2011, as I entered my fifth year of study in a doctoral program in religious studies at an Ivy League university in New York. I had recently moved to Taiwan to conduct research for my dissertation on Chinese Buddhist deathbed culture.

That fall, I began to feel a yearning: an anxious, unsettling, *gnawing* yearning bubbling up from deep within me. Around that time I often wrote in my journal that I felt on the brink of bursting, that I had unnamable things inside me that wanted to break out, that I felt on the verge of some sort of epiphany.

I didn't understand what these feelings meant or where they came from. I hadn't been consciously struggling with any deep ideas or questions that would cause me to feel this way. I was just chugging along with my life, working on my dissertation.

Not very happily, mind you. I cruised along on neutral.

Graduate studies were not the only thing unsettling me during that period. I was also in a long-distance relationship with a beautiful man I had met only a few months earlier while climbing a mountain in the outskirts of Taipei. We fell in love quickly. And then the dirty work of *nurturing* love commenced.

As the relationship developed, my internal mirrors began to encroach and surround me. I began to see flaws and wounds in me that I never dared to acknowledge before. I often projected them onto my partner. We struggled, I cried, and we held on to the hope that love would conquer all.

And so life went on like this for the next several months. I moved in slow motion through a spin cycle of joy, sadness, laughter, anger, light and darkness. It was a cycle which I felt I had little control over. The yearning, the uncomfortable whispering in my soul, grew.

In the springtime, things began to shift.

The shift was sparked by Joseph Campbell and the PBS series *The Power of Myth*. I was in genuine awe of this man: his wisdom, his light-heartedness, and the magical stories he wove. He told of the mystery and beauty of life as a human being on Earth, despite the suffering and fear and death. He seemed to embrace *everything*. The light and the darkness. Joyfully.

This was like a foreign concept to me at the time. I was raised with a strict sense of right and wrong, good and bad. The good was accepted and praised; the bad was rejected and condemned. My study of Buddhism, up until that point, rather than loosening those iron boundaries, tightened them. I mistakenly used Buddhism as a way to measure and judge the world rather than as a way to understand and embrace it.

Joseph Campbell inspired me to face my own darkness with compassion. Paradoxically, at the moment I resolved to see my darkness, a small light in my heart switched on and a barely perceivable stream of relief slowly crept in. I stopped trying to be "good" or "perfect". I slept in. I slacked on my graduate work. I drank and smoked and spent more time with friends. I began to dance—alone in my apartment—all the time. My music of choice was *Florence and the Machine*. It was fierce and pulsating and released animalistic energies in me I didn't know I had.

I sensed my mind begin to expand during this time, but it was not the joyful expansion I would come to experience a year later. Rather, it was confusing and heavy. I knew I was changing, but I didn't understand what I was changing from or what I was transforming into. My nights were often sleepless. A cloud of questions about myself and the world hovered above my pillow, but I could not find the words to articulate them.

In April of 2012 I went to visit my partner in Israel. We went to see a kind energy healer who placed her hands above my heart and spoke words I will never forget: *"It's like you're afraid of living."*

The floodgates opened. I cried like never before. I did not logically comprehend what her words meant, but I felt their meaning pierce my soul.

I saw clearly for the first time ever that I was not living the life I was born to live. I was hiding.

I finally understood those autumn pangs of yearning, those feelings of being on the verge of something huge, the tension enveloping my body. They were all harbingers of this realization.

After this encounter in Israel, I felt like a wild woman unleashed on a mission. I returned first to Taipei then home to New York for the summer. There was fire in my eyes. I wanted desperately to understand why I had been living like this for so long: closed, scared.

That hot summer, I threw myself into a feverish and not-so-graceful search for clarity. I devoured information on energy, healing, Jungian thought, dreams, and spiritual and personal development. I began seeing a therapist who forever changed my life. I dove into my complex relationship with my parents, particularly with my mother. I started observing my emotions and judgments more closely. And I tried my damnedest to let go of my rigid distinctions between good and bad.

By September 2012, as planned, I returned to Taipei to continue my dissertation research. Yes, despite all this personal work, I still managed to avoid facing the thing that was arguably at the center of my life: the Ph.D.

And so, that fall, I resumed gathering research material, reading, translating, analyzing, and writing. I felt a bit lighter overall, but soon enough, I felt that sluggish, chugging motion return. Finally, on February 2, 2013, the engine blew out.

As I sat in front of my laptop doing dissertation work, I suddenly felt mentally and physically incapable of typing another single word. I sat there pouting, half-waiting for the moment to pass. When similar rebellious pangs had struck me in the past, my mighty mind would kick into high gear, propelling me forward with commands like *"Just get it done. It will be over soon. You should be grateful you get to do this. There are so many less fortunate people out there."*

But this time my mind fell silent. Even more startlingly, it actually got on board with my heart, and together they shouted: *"Stop!"*

I chose to listen. I stopped.

Then I contemplated a question that an amazing coach had posed to me a week before: *"If you really loved yourself, what would you do?"*

I sat with this question for a few moments, and I then found myself typing out the answer: *"I would quit school and go on a soul journey. Bardo."*

In the Buddhist tradition, bardo is the intermediate state between birth and death: the pivotal, and sometimes terrifying, period during which a soul searches for what is to be her new existence.

I thought to myself, *"I need to die to my former self before I can be reborn."*

And so I chose death, with the deep faith that I would emerge again. Perhaps this time as my true self.

I decided to embark on a forty-nine-day bardo journey. No more school work, no more stressing about the future, no more being haunted by my past, no more bullshitting myself.

My personal intention for the journey was to learn to love myself.

My soul adventure began on the first day of the Chinese New Year. The year of the snake, a time to shed the past and begin again.

On my journey . . .

> I began to listen to my heart.
> I renewed my love of writing.
> I cultivated the relationship with my amazing partner.
> I started training as a life coach.
> I discovered the power of prayer.
> I began to release myself from the grip of my parents.
> I danced and practiced yoga regularly.
> I nurtured my feminine energies.
> I faced my irrational feelings of guilt, of being a "bad person".
> I began to uncover my unique gifts.
> I worked actively with my dreams.
> I began to journey with sacred plants.
> I followed my bliss even though I was often afraid.

Most importantly, I learned to love myself for exactly who I am in this very moment. Before bardo, I could hardly say the words "I love myself" out loud.

I emerged from bardo on March 30, 2013. There were no bells and whistles accompanying my return to life. No jolt of enlightenment. No fireworks. But I was also no longer the woman I was before the death of me. I finally felt a genuine sense of self. A self that I loved and respected. A self that was joyful. A self that was on a path to freedom.

Lest my journey strike you as a self-indulgent vacation from life, I assure you it was not easy. On the contrary, I think it's easier for people to remain on neutral, chugging along the same old tracks they dug out for themselves long ago. There is safety in the familiar. Stepping off the tracks takes courage.

The death of me was a conscious choice. The death of me plunged my soul into a journey through bardo. The death of me birthed me back into *life*. Beautiful, maddening, breathtaking, painful, wondrous life.

A closing message from above for my fellow journeyers who are reading with an open heart, shared with immense love and light:

The world is waking up now. I know you feel it too. There is suffering—so much suffering—but it is going to get better. We must plant the seeds now and prepare the ground. In times of despair, remember love. Beauty. Rainbows. We all come from the same source, a place of love, and we chose to come here freely. Each human is special, powerful, and has a unique role to play on this Earth. The most beautiful gift we can give ourselves and the planet is to discover who we truly are and to live from that place of genuine knowing. Trust that you are so, so loved. This is only the beginning.

About the Author

Stephanie Lin is a writer, personal coach, and spiritual construction worker. A native New Yorker, she holds an M.A. and M.Phil in Religion from Columbia University. Using her gift of intuiting the struggles of others, her mission is to guide awakening men and women to unbind themselves from fear, embark on a personal bardo journey, and create a conscious, soul-driven, and joyful life. Her compassionate and practical coaching style is tailored to each unique individual and involves a combination of thought work, meditation and prayer, body movement, and the wisdom and healing practices of world spiritual traditions.

http://www.stephanieylin.com

LIFE RESTORED

Tracey Templeman

It's the end of summer 2009. I'm living in an amazing two-storey timber home that my husband and I bought twelve months ago, just seven hundred meters from the beautiful beaches of the Sunshine Coast. I have just set up my new home business in the front garage. A gorgeous little hair salon I decorated myself.

Wow! My manifesting has really started to happen faster and very accurately, I think to myself. *I love the techniques I'm using to create change; they are so simple yet very powerful. I love living here, walking to the beach every day, and living in a community that feels safe. Sunshine, birds chirping, children playing in the streets. How blessed am I? I manifested it all. Every little detail is perfect!*

Well, not quite.

I was not happy at all. I was miserable, sick, and self-medicating.

Why? Why am I so sick? What is my body trying to tell me? I've manifested everything I wanted. Wasn't this what I asked for?

Yet, the reality was, I didn't want it.

The man I had manifested and married just six months ago was possessive and controlling, and he drank in excess nearly every night. He then had angry emotional outbursts. We had no friends, no social life, no fun, and no laughs. Just tears all the time. Silently, I cried myself to sleep every night, screaming to myself, "I want out." I was a prisoner in my own nightmare.

What had happened?

I pulled out the "vision" I had written in my journal about the man I wanted to manifest and read it: "Tall. Strong. Handsome. Green eyes." *(Hmm . . . very accurate.)*

"Loves and worships me." *(Oh! Whoops! Worships me? Not a good idea.)*

"Playful. Loved and accepted my four children, Financially secure, Had his own toys." *(I meant man toys—not the toys he sold on eBay.)*

It turned out I wasn't clear enough at all. I mean what are the chances? Right?

Toys?!

Well, all I can say is "Be careful what you wish for." *Really careful,* because the Universe delivers.

I held my intention and vision, and then *bang!* The Universe gave it to me in a painful way.

So, why was I so sick?

Alarm bells were going off in my head. I had been here before: in a destructive, abusive relationship.

What do I do? I cried until I realized I had to be true to my heart and soul. All this time, I wasn't being true. And *that's* why I was so sick. My body was shaking me and telling me to *get out now!*

So I sat there, pulled out my journal, and thought very clearly about what I truly desired in a relationship and how I wanted my life. And then I began to write. . . .

I want a man who understands me and accepts me for who I am. A man on a spiritual journey to join me in learning and growing together.

I want passion in life, in love and in a cause. Fun, laughter and tears of joy!

I want to travel the world together and explore life. To share my wildest dreams and desires and be heard!

I want him to love me with all his heart and to be my best friend and confidant. Someone I could share my deepest desires and darkest moments.

Quite simply, I wanted true love.

This, I realized I had never felt before.

I sat back and read what I wrote. I knew now that I had to be careful what I wished for. To make it clear and precise.

The Universe will always hear you loud and clear! And it will deliver, sometimes really fast, when you put it out there.

So I took my new desires, held them to my heart, and felt them deep within my soul. I breathed all of it in—slowly and deliberately— and said a little prayer: "Please, God, I deserve more. I deserve to be happy and I am willing to love myself now."

It is time to step up to myself and offer the unconditional love that I need. It is time to put myself first no matter what; otherwise, no one else would.

And so it was.

I placed my letter away inside a deck of angel cards I had hidden in a drawer. Pulling myself up off the floor, I took a deep breath.

It is time to end the pain and suffering.

I had only been married six months. And to be true to myself, I needed to end it before it ended me. After all, I did have four kids who needed a roof over their heads, and I had just started my business from home. My vision was what drove me. So I started the "clear and precise" manifesting process of everything I wanted.

"I'll need a house, a shop to lease for my business, and money."

Using my vision mapping techniques, I started to create all of it.

It must have been a strong desire twenty years earlier because that was exactly where the Universe directed me. I was driving with a friend and we were heading to look at premises for lease, when all of a sudden she said, "Wait! Go left! I want to go see my boyfriend!"

"Really? Now?" I asked. "Okay! Left turn it is." Then I saw it—a big red sign: *FOR LEASE*. It was on an old white Spanish-looking building on the water front. And it was not there the day before!

I pulled over and got the number off the sign, called them straight away, and said, "I will take the shop on the esplanade, please. Where do I sign?"

It was perfect and just as I had imagined. Things were on the move.

Look at how the Universe provides for you when you love yourself enough and believe it will happen. Trust and follow your heart. It will never let you down. I knew in my heart that getting married was not the answer, but I wanted to be loved so much. If only I realized I had to love myself first before anyone else would love me the way I desired. My husband was just a reflection of how I was treating myself, no more, no less.

I decided to stay in the house until we settled and he moved out. My life had taken a turn. I was starting to feel stronger, and the pain was leaving me: that spark of life that shines bright when you are true to yourself was poking through—and it was infectious.

It was late afternoon and I was finishing up for the day when another client came for a haircut. I'll never forget that day he pulled up in his old Holden Ute (I love old classic cars). As I looked out the glass doors, down the driveway, my heart fluttered and buzzed, my stomach turned to butterflies, as he stepped out of the car. He came inside and sat down, and I started to cut his hair.

Why am I so nervous? I'm never nervous. What is going on?!

The chemistry was electrifying. He had such a beautiful smile and soft gentle eyes. He wasn't able to have his hair washed that day due to an injury he sustained while skydiving.

"I was going to skydive for my fortieth," I told him.

"I'll take you; when's your birthday?"

"August," I replied.

"Mine too! What date?"

"28th."

"No way! Mine too! Well, we should definitely do it this year—not next," said the man who's chute did not open!

And then, the haircut was over and he was gone. *Wow! What just happened? What was that feeling? That buzz of excitement?*

In twenty years, I had never felt that way for a client. *Okay, back to life, miss! You have a house to sell and you've only just left your ex-husband. You can't move that fast. . . .*

Or could I?

I later found out that one of my clients' local clients was boarding him at her place and sent him my way. And she was just around the corner.

More excitement! That meant he would need another haircut and I would see him again!

Four weeks later, there he was at my door, looking more handsome than ever and smelling delish. We chatted and flirted, and I could not keep my hands from shaking while cutting his hair. I thought he would see my nerves for sure. *Ask him out. Go on.*

You can do it!

No way! I'm not doing that! (I listened more to that voice in my head as my higher self often knew best.) I couldn't ask him to chicken. Off he went again.

Now what do I do?

As the days went by, he played on my mind all the time. It seemed he was under my skin. I thought he would've called me by now to ask me out. I was sure I read the signs properly: he was flirting. "Maybe he has a girlfriend? A wife? I didn't see a ring on his finger or—*Bingo! I have a ring on my finger! He thinks I'm married. Damn! I am still married—separated but married. Time to take the ring off. Does that mean he's not going to call me? What to do? What to do? Breathe! Just breathe!*

I was going to have to call him. I just couldn't wait for the next haircut. It was too far away. And what if he found someone else? So much fear came up.

What's the worst that could happen?

So, I called him to ask him out. My heart was pounding out of my chest. And guess what? He said, "Yes!" (followed by me squealing and dancing around the room after I hung up!) I felt like a child at Christmas; the feeling was truly new and exciting. I had been married twice and not once could I remember feeling so excited.

Soon after, we met for coffee; afterwards, we went to dinners and then movies, beach walks, Sunday drives, and long weekends. We even went overseas together. Our romance gradually blossomed and grew. We took it slow and grew to know each other like best friends only can. We planned our life together—and then our wedding.

Finally, I was truly in love with all my heart and soul. Just like I had so recently intended! And we ended up marrying in the heart of Sedona, Arizona, on a cliff overlooking a valley: one the world's most spiritual places. It was the most amazing day of my life.

I knew deep down inside that I would find him. I just had to believe and follow my heart.

Now, one year to the day, we are about to renew our vows again here in Australia with friends and family. Plus, I am heading overseas again and following my passion as a writer and designer. Just like I had intended.

Life is truly a blessing, and you can manifest all that you desire.

About the Author

Tracey Templeman is a rockstar entrepreneur who is one part renegade bohemian and one part super savvy business chick. She is at the frontline of the wave of new empowerpreneurs leading the paradigm shift to new soul consciousness. An inspirational writer, artist, author, and founder of "Shifting with Tracey", her laser-sharp wit and soulful softness will leave you breathless.

http://www.traceytempleman.com

THE MANIFESTING COURSE

Looking for Guidance?

TheManifestingCourse.com is the place to go to discover an *ancient manifesting technique* you've probably never even heard of before. Join *thousands of inspired people* who LOVE **The Manifesting Workbook** and receive weekly devotions, heart-candy + wisdom from bestselling author, entrepreneur + publisher, and lover of metaphysics, **Sarah Prout.**

www.TheManifestingCourse.com

"I LOVE this book Sarah! I did the 55x5 process straight away and it worked like magic! I am seeing results from doing that process everyday! Thank you for sharing it with us all!"
~ Claire Camden-Burch

"I loved the free manifesting e-book, I went through my entire wardrobe and drawers and have cleared out a lot of things I don't wear for a car boot sale next weekend. Since then I have had an offer to date from 3! Different men and also attracted 2 new client enquiries and had a publication in a magazine! Amazing."
~Wendy Fry

"I only recently discovered Sarah and her amazing work, but saw results on my very first day of following her techniques! I am very impressed and can't wait to read her other work. Sarah knows what she's talking about and her tools and tips are tailored exactly to bring you the best possible outcome. Thank you, Sarah! :)"
~ Violet Flame

"The vision board process is awesome! I've been tweaking it, and love how it's growing and evolving with me, as my desires and goals change. Seeing amazing results with this already."
~ Zuri Eberhart

SHARE YOUR STORY AND
JOIN THE COMMUNITY

Have a Story to Share?

Everyone has a story, including you! With several *Adventures in Manifesting* titles in production each year, we are constantly looking for more journeys to share. Ask yourself, *what story of mine could change someone's life?*

Whether you have a story to tell or lesson to teach, we're listening. Share yours and get the guide to writing and submitting your chapter here:

www.AdventuresInManifestingSeries.com

The stories we keep an eye out for are any that has to do with manifesting (success, spirituality, health, happiness, wealth, love, prosperity, inner guidance, achieving dreams, overcoming obstacles, etc.)

If chosen as a top submission, we will get in touch directly to invite you to be a part of one of our next *Adventures in Manifesting* titles.

Feeling Inspired?

We always love to hear how our readers were touched, inspired, or changed by the stories shared. If you'd like to share your experience with us, send us an e-mail to:

feedback@adventuresinmanifesting.org

CONSCIOUS PUBLISHING
FOR CONSCIOUS AUTHORS

Discover the New Empowered Publishing Solution Conscious Authors are Using to Create Beautiful Books and Share Their Message With the World

Adventures in Manifesting isn't the only way to get your message out there. You can do it with your own book through one of the world's fastest growing self-publishing brands, Verbii.

www.Verbii.com

Soon you'll understand why authors worldwide are turning to Verbii to publish their book in an empowered way... without the confusion, without the contracts, and without the limitations.

Experience the easy, game-changing book publishing solution you've been waiting for by going to www.Verbii.com *now*.

MORE ADVENTURES IN MANIFESTING TITLES

--iBooks and Kindle--

All Älska Publishing titles can be found through the www.AdventuresInManifestingSeries.com portal or requested from your local bookstore (and found through online bookstores as well).

Books

Adventures in Manifesting: Success and Spirituality

Adventures in Manifesting: Health and Happiness

Adventures in Manifesting: Passion and Purpose

Adventures in Manifesting: Healing from Within

Adventures in Manifesting: Love and Oneness

Adventures in Manifesting: Soulful Relationships

Adventures in Manifesting: Conscious Business

The Kindle and iBooks

Each of the Adventures in Manifesting titles above can also be purchased via the Amazon Kindle or iTunes iBook formats via AdventuresInManifesting.org.

SHARE WITH LOVE

Is someone you know on the deep and profound journey within? If so, be sure to share with them the entire book or specific stories you intuitively felt would resonate with them.

The meaning of Älska is "to Love" (it's a Swedish Verb!).

The *chapters* were written with Love.

The *book* was published with Love.

And now it's up to you to *share* with Love.

From the bottom of our hearts and deepest depths of our soul, thank you, thank you, thank you.

With Love & Gratitude,

Älska

http://www.AlskaPublishing.com

ABOUT THE AUTHORS

SEAN PATRICK SIMPSON

Sean is the co-founder of both Älska Publishing and Verbii.com who thrives on leading the Älska team and growing the company with his love, Sarah. A musician and singer at heart, Sean has had his music played in over 30 countries after creating an album for the Fox Sports networks. If you look closely enough, you might even notice him singing a little dittie in the movie *Anchorman*.

SARAH PROUT

Sarah's love for metaphysics, design, and business empowerment shines through in her writing and teachings. Since 2006, Sarah has built an impressive international media and client portfolio inspiring people to create their own reality. Sarah reaches over 55,000 followers in over 24 countries around the globe with heartfelt, vibrant, and empowering advice about love, business, and style.

You can connect with Sarah and Sean at any of the sites you feel most inspired to discover.

http://www.AlskaPublishing.com (Home-site)

http://www.Verbii.com (Conscious Publishing for Conscious Authors)

http://www.AdventuresInManifestingSeries.com (Home of the Bestselling Series)

http://www.SarahProut.com (Lifestyle Business for Female Entrepreneurs)